DATE DUE

20 '76			
MAY 24 '77	JUL 23 2004		
JY 21 '81			
14 '82	RECEIVED		
	JUL 22 2004		

GAYLORD PRINTED IN U.S.A.

Religious Experience Series

Edward J. Malatesta, S.J., General Editor

Volume 1 Jesus in Christian Devotion and Contemplation
Volume 2 A Christian Anthropology
Volume 3 The Revelations of Divine Love of Julian of Norwich
Volume 4 How to Pray Today
Volume 5 Imitating Christ
Volume 6 Paths to Contemplation
Volume 7 Celibacy for Our Times

Religious Experience Series

Volume 6

Paths to Contemplation

by

Yves Raguin, S.J.
Translated by Paul Barrett, O.F.M. Cap.

ABBEY PRESS
St. Meinrad, Indiana 47577
1974

BV
5091
C7R313
1974
C.1

#11 20037

BQT
2469
R3.

Paths to Contemplation is the English translation of *Chemins de la contemplation,* which was originally published by Desclée De Brouwer, Paris, France, 1969.

Nihil obstat: Father Peter Rogers, O.F.M. Cap.
Censor deputatus

Imprimi potest: Father Anthony Boran, O.F.M. Cap.
Min. Prov. Hib.

December 8, 1973

Library of Congress Catalog Card Number: 74-84160
ISBN: 0-87029-032-0
© 1974 by Edward J. Malatesta, S.J.
Printed in the U.S.A.

Scripture quotations are from *The New American Bible* © 1970 by the Confraternity of Christian Doctrine, Washington, D.C., and used by permission.

Preface

This is not a systematic treatise on the spiritual life but a guide to those who are engaged in that life. That is why we have presented the material in the form of short, inter-connected chapters, a manner of presentation that is derived directly from traditional Chinese pedagogy, for, in the classical Chinese treatises, the would-be disciple is initiated by someone who himself has had a spiritual experience and who believes that the pupil can make progress only by repetition and silence. Strictly speaking, each chapter in this book is a day's full ration.

We shall touch only lightly upon certain questions which really require development at length and which are dealt with in more complete, systematic works. And even in such works it is not a matter of saying everything but of giving a start to the reader, the disciple, who will then follow, not the teaching of his master, but the development of his own experience.

The book is divided into two parts, the first depicting a spiritual journey, following the normal curve of the development of contemplation, while the second part deals with general questions. We portray the soul as allowing God to take over its direction gradually. We have deliberately simplified the process of the soul's passing from so-called ordinary prayer to the mystical life, and we have described only the more characteristic stages of that life.

The chapters in this book were written in a matter of days, as they flowed from the pen, and are not so much the result of knowledge acquired from books as the reflection of the spiritual experiences of a great number of souls encountered by the author over a period of twenty-five years.

Accordingly, we dedicate these pages to all those who thus helped to write them.

Yves Raguin, S.J.
Taichung, Taiwan

ALUMNI MEMORIAL LIBRARY
389383 Creighton University
Omaha, Nebraska 68178

Contents

Introduction

As we said, this is not a treatise; instead, it is a path cut through the thickets of theories and methods and deliberately made wide to meet the demands of freedom of spirit. Those who have already had an experience of God will find additional light shed on their own spiritual life, while others will discover the beginnings of an interior liberation that will make them more skilful in perceiving the work of grace in their souls. As we noted in the preface, those short chapters are the reflection of the experiences of a great number of souls, experiences which are all fundamentally alike in that they show the progressive unveiling of God's action in the very act of prayer right up to its full blossoming in the most intimate relationship that can exist between God and man. Hence these *Paths* are a sort of mystical road-map, laid out as simply as possible. The theme is not a complicated one. The method used by a soul that engages in contemplation seems to be, at the beginning, completely human, but little by little God shows His presence in that soul, and this presence increases until it absorbs into itself all human activity, without, however, rendering that activity fruitless.

This short volume does not say everything on the subject since it presupposes in the reader either an experience of God or the desire to have such an experience. Nor can this book be read merely passively since anyone who treads these *Paths* is on the march, moving forward, longing for contemplation and aware that he is being called thereto. Hence, too, the style of the book is necessarily terse, for it is not meant to stir the emotions but to clarify ideas. Most of the chapters are concise and, on the surface, impersonal descriptions of experiences that are actually too powerful and too deep to be described fully. That is why the proper way to read these pages is not at the superficial level of the words, but at the level of the heart, the spirit, the substantial being, where God speaks in actions and sometimes in words.

The first draft of the book was written as it flowed from the pen at the end of the year 1965, and it was given its final shape in the following year in Taiwan (Formosa). *Paths* was not written especially for the Chinese but rather for all those who can profit from it in their search for God. It would be quite presumptuous, if not useless, for a European to attempt to write a treatise on the spiritual life for the Chinese alone; yet it is clear that, when an author has spent many years in China and has tried to understand Chinese culture, his writing will take on a certain Oriental coloration. *Paths* is a work that has been derived from the West and from the East, too, without, however, the elements drawn from either being simply placed side by side, with the result that the book truly integrates both cultures and, in its own small way, tries to be the beginning of a more perfect blending of both.

The experience traced out in this book is a typically Christian one and is meant to be neither a compromise nor a syncretism because both the one and the other are always accomplished on the surface alone. A solution in depth demands a fundamental assumption. Now, the ultimate solution can only be Christ, the God-Man, and, in final analysis, all other solutions derive their efficacy from Him and are thus integrated into the structure of the whole, which cannot but be one in an infinite diversity. In this perspective, the Christian spiritual experience must be presented as the one and only solution. Indeed, the Buddha, for example, positively refused to give solutions to the essential problems of man's relationship to God and even to the problem of the very existence of God and fulfilled his responsibilities by presenting himself simply as a teacher of doctrine, whereas Christ accomplished His mission by declaring that He was God and by dying for doing so.

I realize that this attitude will appear too radical and quite disdainful of the religious positions of others, but should respect for the beliefs of others make us withhold judgment? As a matter of fact, I believe that there exists a reality which not all men have the same capability of discovering, and this is the criterion which must finally be applied in all sincerity when examining, as we are doing here, what Buddha and Christ claimed to be.

Those who have only a superficial knowledge of eastern Asia may, now and then in the course of reading this book, find that they are puzzled either by the presentation of the problems or by the questions raised, while those who are more familiar with Asia will see that we constantly allude to and recall the most cherished theories of the East. *Paths* is not an exotic, much less an esoteric, way of going toward God.

The East and the West influence each other profoundly without always being aware of doing so. During the period in which the East was dominated by the West, the East accepted an amazing number of innovations, both technical and intellectual, while still retaining the conviction that it was spiritually superior to the West. This is, of course, an over-simplification of the case, yet this is not the place to go into greater detail. What is certain, however, is that the spiritual and spiritualistic currents of the East have had an increasing influence on the Western world, and these currents flowed in to fill a void that was made even deeper by the present activistic attitude of a great number of Christians who have abandoned this interior domain where man can have access to true life. But—and this is the point that interests us here—the West did accept the contributions of the East and adapted them to its own mentality. In Taiwan there is a Buddhist review for students which is devoted to this new form of Buddhism being elaborated by Westerners. The same phenomenon may be observed in the transformation of Chinese Maoism into French Maoism, for example. In the same way, the East reacts to Western influences, but, in both cases, the original doctrines are changed as the result of an inevitable distortion. It is thus that the threads of thought from East and West become interwoven in preparation for a unification of all human thought on the most evolved level of culture. And it is precisely one aspect, among others, of this gigantic confrontation of cultures that we intend to present here.

The general line of approach that we have adopted is in agreement with the Chinese mentality inasmuch as that mentality integrates the spiritual life into the totality of man and of the universe. Western man's separation of these elements is only temporary, and he who has found God is he who, like the holy men of ancient China, has penetrated to the heart of all the mysteries of the universe and has succeeded in establishing a perfect fraternal relationship with all men. The saint's union with God unites him with all beings, and his freedom surpasses the freedom which the Taoist holy man could even hope for. This great harmony which crowns the efforts of those who follow these *Paths* blends in with the harmony of all creation so dear to Chinese tradition, and it does so by reaching back to the ultimate principle of things. The saint, alert to the pulse-beat of the universe, adapts himself to the very rhythm of the Creator as He unceasingly brings that universe into existence.

In these pages, the journey toward God is always presented in a human context, for man progresses toward the discovery of God along his own special interior path. All through the journey, the focus of our attention will be the action of God upon a particular type of man, the Christian man, and so we shall gradually come to see how God reveals Himself in this man. But such a journey is different from that of a Buddhist, for whom creation is purely an illusion from which he must become detached, whereas the Christian detachment demanded of the contemplative is of quite a different type. The reality of the divine presence gives all created things their truth. The presence of the divine does not annihilate the created world but allows it to exist for itself, and this manner of being becomes at the same time a sign of Him who exists *of* Himself.

Hence the philosophy of being upon which this book is based cannot but be both a surpassing of the Buddhist theories and, at the same time, a striking encounter with the more objective approach of Taoism. Therefore an exposition of the Christian journey to God implies a judgment of the Buddhist position, and this is also true of the search for God by the positive and negative ways. In Buddhism, there can be question only of the negative way, since, for the Buddhist, all creation is merely an illusion, and since the sole reality is the ultimate Reality, which reveals itself only as a "void" in the universal void. But the Christian, in his advance toward contemplation, begins by making a statement about God which he must later deny in order to go beyond it and take the next step.

It is obviously wrong to interpret the term "void," as used by the Buddhists, in the very negative sense in which we use it, and it is no less erroneous to think that they employ this word to indicate what we understand when we speak of "God" or the "Absolute Being." It is true that the way in which one envisions the divinity does not change the nature of that Divinity, but it is incorrect to think that all men—Hindus, Buddhists and we Christians—have the same basic belief about the nature of God. That is why, in several places, we draw attention to the differences between Christianity and certain schools of Buddhism.

It follows that the affirmative philosophy of being upon which this book is based is already in itself an answer to the Buddhist theory of the illusory nature of reality. What we say about effort and grace is to be understood in relation to Buddhist theories as carried to the extreme in the schools of the Hînayâna,[1] which deny all cooperating assistance on the part of the impersonal Absolute, the basis of reality. Christ's role as Mediator, Way, Life and Light, as both God and man at the same time, stands out in bold relief against the background of the Buddhist theories of the non-mediation of the Buddha. Mention is often made of the rigor of spiritual methods which impose a heavy burden on the contemplative—a reference to certain methods employed in Christianity but also to the asceticism demanded by certain Zen exercises. But to base the whole success of the spiritual enterprise on a controllable technique would be to constrain the soul to the use of very strict methods, and, indeed, we often hear mystical states described as if they could be produced almost at will, provided one used the appropriate means. On this point our views are quite clear: human techniques can bring about certain states, but these states can have nothing mystical about them in the Christian sense of the term.

This question is extremely important. A mysticism based on techniques such as those used in Yoga or Zen can lead only to a perception of the self. It is true that this perception can be such that one's personality is revealed to its very depths while, at the same time, it opens out to embrace the whole of creation. But if such a mysticism does not open out onto the the Infinite, it is not mysticism, and it merely shuts man up within an intuition which, however, can have all the appearances of going beyond all sense perception. In Christian mysticism, faith is essential and is both the driving power behind the soul's progress and the light that guides it on its journey. Even the most sublime and the most profound mystical states are only a springboard which launches man toward Him who is always beyond the created world. It is no longer a question here of resting in a happy state of presence and of being, because one must always go beyond any state that man can attain by himself; and conversely, from the Christian contemplative's very first step, this presence of faith and of grace renders less necessary the refined techniques designed to lead to ecstasy. Thus faith frees the Chrisitan contemplative from a terrible constraint.

There is another, more important point that must be stressed if this book is to be properly understood. The dominant tendency among the contemplatives of Asia is toward loss of self in the divine, and since this divine is impersonal, it cannot accept man as a person, with the result that the self is lost in the fundamental and essential reality. How could it be otherwise for the Buddhist when the "I" that is seen has no real substance? This "I" must be reabsorbed, as it were, in order to allow the "real I" to appear, although this "real I" is not personal either. According to the theory that is most widely accepted among the Hindus, the *âtman,* which is the personal soul, is one with the *Brahman,* the Absolute. In this view, as in Buddhism, the person disappears, and it cannot be otherwise since the Absolute is conceived as being impersonal.

The Christian viewpoint is quite different from this. God is personal in the sense that He is "Persons," not just one Person but three; and even more than that, these Persons are relationhips, and each one of these "Person-relationships" is the One God, the Absolute, the Unconditioned. This mystery was formulated in this way only after long study and application of the words and actions of Christ, and the present formulation may perhaps one day give place to others which will complete it. But for the moment we can use it because it takes account of the Gospel data and allows us to center the attention of faith on the mystery itself. It would not be very rational to be put off by the systematic expositions of the doctrine of the Trinity, for the important point is the reality of the fact of the Trinity. When, like the Hindus and Buddhists, we have first tried to reconcile the irreconcilable and then face up boldly to the mystery of the Trinity, we find that the mystery itself is the solution. It is sufficient to follow the teaching of Christ, which clearly shows that He wants us to be one with Him as He is one with His Father and that He asks us to submit to losing ourselves in Him in order to lose ourselves in God. And we know that by "losing" ourselves in Him, we become sons of God, in Him and by Him. To the extent that we "lose" ourselves in God, we personalize ourselves in the manner of the Divine Persons; and even more than that, we personalize ourselves to the same extent as we divinize ourselves, and as we increasingly share in the divine nature, the love that exists between us and God grows ever greater until we are transformed into Him and become more truly persons.

It is precisely this relationship of love which is the special mark of Christianity. Hinduism knows other forms of love which approach this concept, but Buddhism has nothing similar. It is true that some people interpret the Buddhist's love for the Buddha Amida (Amitabha) in an almost Christian sense. In this relatively late version of Buddhism, the devout Buddhist does, in fact, dedicate himself to Amida as to a savior in whom he puts all his faith, but this concept does not meet the demands of the perfect interrelationship of love. Buddhism remains a religion of knowledge and compassion, whereas Christianity has united knowledge and love. Moreover, the Christian definition of God is love, while in Buddhism, in which the person has no real substance, love cannot exist.

Since this book was written in the Orient, it is natural that it should stress the meaning of union with God in a context of impersonality. Moreover, the Christian mystical experience often arises in this way, for God shows Himself as an impersonal force working in Nature and in the soul itself, and even love itself frequently appears thus. Hence we thought it necessary to bring together the great stream of negative mysticism from the West and similar streams from the mysticism of the Orient, and in this way we can perhaps counterbalance the peculiarly Western temptation to over-personalize God, on the one hand, and to believe, on the other hand, that it is possible to encompass Him in a system of definitions. The great mystics and the great theologians did not fall into these traps; quite the contrary. But we do know that this tendency has impoverished contemplation in the West. In addition, a proper understanding of the Christian mystery can make God the goal and culmination of a contemplation which, for the majority of Orientals, is lost in a hopeless "unknowing."

We could have inserted here copious footnotes referring to Chinese authors or to the specific doctrines that are widespread in the East, but that would have given a false impression of the objectives of this book, which is meant to be an interweaving of the teachings of East and West and not a series of snippets put together with scissors and paste. The book is all of a piece, and the elements that go to make it have been lived in a unified experience. However, later on I hope to write another, more technical, work in which I shall try to correlate, in their original context, the basic beliefs of the different religious trends. In this way it will be possible to arrive at a comparison of these diverse positions. But in the present volume the important thing is to maintain the unity of the way of contemplation while assimilating into it everything possible. Thus we will be able to mark out other paths to God in the context of the religions of Asia, a procedure which has the advantage of having been lived and of being still lived, and which, therefore, can help others towards future religious experiences. At any rate, we do know that *Paths,* circulated in manuscript form, has already revealed to many souls the way God leads them and guides them to Him.

As I have said, this book was written without any particular reader, Western or Oriental, in mind, and actually it can help both types of reader simply by the way it develops. Thus, for example, apprehending God beyond all possible formulating is obviously reminiscent of the opening sentences of the *Tao-te-ching,* which is the gospel of the Taoist tradition and whose title means *The Way and Its Power*:

> The Way that can be told is not an unvarying way;
> The names that can be named are not unvarying names:
> It was from the Nameless that Heaven and Earth sprang.[2]

Yet the doctrine expressed here is that of the great Christian mystics. The God in search of whom the contemplative sets out is already within him and in the whole universe. This is a Christian teaching but it is also one which corresponds perfectly to a fundamental attitude of the Chinese who, all unconsciously, live in harmony with the entire universe. This idea underlies the contemplation of the artist, the poet and of every man who is aware that he is living in the heart of the universe. The holy man who grasps this harmony perfectly is sensitive to all the influences of Heaven and earth. Even when he rejects this harmony intellectually, he cannot but be vitally aware of it. From the position which each man must occupy in the universe, he reaches his destiny in communion with the cosmos, and this sharing in the harmony of creation makes him sensitive to the movements of Heaven, of earth and of human groups.

On every page of this book we are dealing with the presence of God in the universe and in the soul of the contemplative. God is present in creation as the life that animates it, and man is plunged into this great river, this ocean, of life. Not even for a moment do we speak about the soul as if it were outside man, or man as outside the universe, or the universe outside God. Yet God remains God, the Infinite Source, so far beyond man's grasp that he can attain Him only in the divine streams that flow from Him, the images that represent Him and the signs of His action. Hence there is no danger that this can be called pantheism. God is in everything, but as a personal Being whose inner life is the relationship of Persons. And no matter how divinized the human soul may be, it is never God; it can never say: "I AM," but only: "I am." God can quite well be immanent to the world because, since He is a Person, He is not encompassed by it, but great as that world is, He goes beyond it.

As it stands, this volume can serve as a guide for readers from both East and West. Certainly, contemplation is not the "in" thing in a society that is sick from its own activism and in which many people regard contemplation as being empty and useless. This is, no doubt, inevitable in the present spiritual context, in which people, when they think of God at all, look upon Him as being, in some vague fashion, the foundation of all things, in somewhat the same way as the Buddhists would define Him if they had to do so. It is alleged that contemplation alienates people from reality, but isn't refusing to examine the very nature of man the only real alienation from reality? We often hear talk of the depths of man's mind and heart, but modern man is shallow. Nevertheless, depth of mind and heart has an attraction for him, but only perhaps to the extent that it does not directly threaten to disturb the even tenor of his accustomed ways. Now, these paths lead through man's heart to reach that which goes to make up his special being. By getting to know his own nature, man opens himself up to that in man himself which is more intimate, more profound and more true than man alone. People seek God in their relationships with others, for who wants to go searching for Him all alone? In this book, we show how man discovers God by discovering what he himself is. In his relationship with God, the individual embraces all mankind in an immense love and, in the end, becomes capable of giving interpersonal relationships their true dimension.

If we take interpersonal relationships as our starting point, we can follow the teaching of the Chinese philosophers. For the Confucians,[3] and for Mei-ti[4] among them, the essential thing is the relationship of man to man, the *jen.* The most profound of the Chinese philosophers saw quite clearly that this virtue of man's love for others could exist only if man attained the perfection of his own nature. That is what Mencius[5] saw and expressed remarkably well, explaining that, if man reflects, he will descend into his own heart, into the essential part of his being, the site and agent of his spiritual life. Therefore, if man descends into his own heart, he will discover his true nature and, in that nature, his relationship to heaven, that is to say, to God. What man must do is reach down into the very depths of his being.

> He who exerts his mind to the utmost knows his nature.
> He who knows his nature knows heaven.[6]

Here again, our *Paths to Contemplation* follow the basic direction of those Chinese philosophers who did not allow themselves to be shut up in a world of merely horizontal relationships and in whose doctrine man's relationship to heaven occupied a privileged place because it is the foundation of all other relationships, so much so that, if it is neglected, all other relationships lose their depth. Then, too, a purely interpersonal relationship ends by destroying itself by emptying the person of that which gives value to the relationship.

Western men of our generation cannot be indifferent to the problems which we pose in this book and to the manner in which we solve them. Our presentation may not appeal to modern tastes, but if we had made such an appeal our main object, it would have detracted from our purpose in writing the book, which was to cut a well-marked path through time, space and everyday life, a path along which the men of today and of tomorrow can journey toward God.

Six months ago, the Chinese edition of this book came off the press. Wherever possible, the translator, Sister Monica Liu, deliberately chose to express the great realities and spiritual experiences in terms that would be understood by non-Christians and that take on their Christian significance in the whole context of the book, becoming clear in the light of each one's experience. This modest volume, such as it is, enters into a great design and strives to be the witness to one experience which, we hope, will give rise to thousands of others. Much has been said about expressing the Christian message in language suitable to the genius of each culture, but this can be done by theologians only if the theological experience has first been lived by spiritual men and if they share this experience with their fellowmen.

Paris, November 21, 1968
Yves Raguin, S.J.

Note: This book is divided into two parts which clearly run parallel to each other. The first part is the more practical, while the second is the more theoretical, and perhaps it may be beneficial to go from one to the other according to the reader's needs, while for some it may even be preferable to begin with the second part.

NOTES TO INTRODUCTION

[1] A Sanskrit word meaning "Little Vehicle" and referring to one of the two great schools of Buddhism, the other being the Mahayâna or "Great Vehicle."

[2] Lao Tzu, *The Way and Its Power,* translated by Arthur Waley (London, Allen and Unwin, 1956), p. 141.

[3] Confucius (551-479 B.C.) is the latinized form of K'ung Fu-tzu, which means "Great Master K'ung." *Tzu,* also spelled *tze* and *tse,* means "philosopher," "scholar" or "master." Confucius was a great humanist who wished to help men to build an earthly city worthy of their unique and fundamental "nobility." He based his teaching on two great principles, *jen* and *li, jen* being man's social aspect. Man has, by his very nature, a relationship to others without which he could not be a man—"Man is a relationship to others." Confucius held that man cannot realize himself without this relationship, which is composed of respect, service and love, and that he must exercise it with those close to him and with his ruler in what Confucius called the "six relationships."

[4] Mei-ti, who probably lived between 480 and 400 B.C., was a "questioning" disciple of Confucius whose six relationships he rejected as being too narrow: instead, he wanted to extend *jen* to the whole world and called on all men to strive directly toward "universal love."

[5] Mencius, the latinized form of Meng-tzu (372-289 B.C.), "Master Meng," was to Confucius what Plato was to Socrates. According to his *Book of Mencius,* which traces his wandering career, he tried to build a society founded on the fundamental truth about man, which is "the nobility of heaven" living "at the bottom of his heart," a nobility that Mencius summed up in a compound expression *Jen-i,* "love-justice," in the name of which he tried to renew men, philosophers and princes. He asked everyone to "think," "reflect," and to go "to the very depths of themselves."

[6] Mencius, *The Book of Mencius,* 7A, 1. Translation by Wing-tsit Chan, in *A Source Book in Chinese Philosophy* (Princeton University Press, 1963), p. 78.

Part One
Paths

Chapter 1

Starting Out in Search of God

If you want to start out in search of God by following the path of contemplation, don't think that you are reaching out for the unreachable. God is already waiting for you. This desire which you have to start searching for Him comes from Him. It is His call. He does not want you to know it yet, but, believe me, this desire comes from Him. He has given you the longing to search for Him; He has, with His own hands, prepared food for your journey, and He has foreseen the stages of that journey. Whether He shows Himself or not is of little importance, for you will find that His attentive love has prepared everything for you, both food and shelter. Perhaps at one point or another you will recognize Him in the breaking of bread. Perhaps He will walk along part of the way with you . . .

You are seeking to attain your God. You wish to know Him with all the strength of your soul and to love Him with all the strength of your heart. It was He whom the saints sought before you did and whom they found. You wish to see your God, to hear Him, to love Him, not, as hitherto, by means of a faith which, even at its best, leaves man with his desire for God unfulfilled, but rather with a new knowledge which the patriarchs, prophets and saints experienced. You want to be able to say "I have seen God . . ."

No one can see God in this world and live, yet only he who sees Him will live. That's a fact: both of these statements are true. You cannot see God; nevertheless, God makes Himself seen. Others before you have sought for Him and found Him. They did not find Him as a result of their own efforts, yet they would never have found Him without those efforts. This desire of yours to find God, which surges from the depths of your heart, which is your own desire and not your neighbor's, which finds its deepest source in you, is a desire which comes from God. This desire carries you toward God, and God is waiting for the desire that inspires you, to become yours to such a degree that it will truly be the desire of your whole being, and only then will He give Himself to you. It is not you who track Him down, who seize Him and force Him to give Himself to You. Oh, no! God does not allow Himself be seized in that way. It is He who makes His presence felt, who reveals Himself and gives Himself to you . . . In order to receive Him and grasp Him, you even need His strength because yours will never be powerful enough.

Perhaps you have already formed quite a clear image of your God. You have read the lives of the saints, especially the lives of the great mystics, and you have elaborated a mental picture of God. You believe that you have a good idea of how He looks, and you have made a mental portrait of Him for yourself. But do not become attached to all that, because you would then be like the two disciples on the road to Emmaus. They thought that Christ would have saved the world in some other way . . . Many people don't seek to see God but try to put a countenance of their own making on Him. God does not have a face. Or rather, He has only one face, the one He took when He became incarnate, and even that face was an obstacle for most of those whom He met on earth.

You are starting out in search of God. You do not know in what guise He will show Himself to you. In all probability,

He won't have a particular countenance, He won't have any name, and you won't be able to find any definition that you will be able to apply to Him when you see Him . . . You are setting out, full of a great desire, but free of all these names, representations, definitions and visions . . . God is God, and He is beyond everything that can be seen of Him. We call Him "God," but in fact, He does not have a name. When Moses asked Him His name, He did not give it but simply said: "I am."

Because He "is," you "are" also, you exist from Him and by Him . . . It is in this bond of being that you will grasp Him . . . beyond everything that can be conceived and said, in being, in the communication of His being that He gives to you.

You are dreaming about receiving great spiritual lights, but perhaps you will have to walk in darkness and through the barren desert. You are dreaming about illumination, and perhaps you will find only black night, but in that night God is: He is there for you.

Even if everybody wanted to start out on the road toward God, in the hope of seeing Him, hearing Him, and touching that which they have already grasped through faith, the earth would still not be changed into one vast monastery. The universe would still be full of human activity. There would still be people who sought solitude, but the mass of humanity would be completely occupied with this earth and with mankind, which had both become transparently full of God's presence and action. Humanity would be both more active and more contemplative, and God would be pleased to come every evening after work to converse with men. The days would not be like those grey Sundays when the Mass seems dreary and the sermon is dull.

Men would still fall and commit sin, but there would be great joy in the excitement of putting the Lord's creation to work, and the accomplishment would belong entirely both to God and to man . . . Undoubtedly this is only a far-off dream for the whole of humanity, which is one more reason why those who feel a desire to see this dream come true should seek even more ardently to behold the face of God.

Many souls seek God, but many more would seek Him if they knew how to go about it. Many have sought Him without finding Him, and some have allowed themselves to be deceived by arid and arduous methods that promised them peace of soul and a very dubious illumination... Yet is there any better teacher than Christ? His method is simple, requiring fewer exercises and more love.

Chapter 2

Beginning the Journey

When you decide to set out in search of God, you must pack your bags, saddle your horse and start on your way. The mountain of God is just barely visible in the distance, and you must be on the road at dawn.

But first you must say goodbye. To whom? To what? To everything—and to nothing. To nothing, because the world that you are leaving will always be there, close to you, in you, until your last breath, and always as close to you as your breath. Although you have rejected and repulsed the world, there is a very good chance that it will rise up again even more vehemently within you. And you must say goodbye to everything, because, when you set out in search of the Absolute, you burn behind you the bridges that connect you with everything that could cause you to turn back, with everything that, in yourself and in created things, tends to become an obstacle to God's action. In the end, you will find that the hardest thing to leave is yourself because the self has a basic need to be independent and is therefore opposed to God.

Finally, leaving the world and self behind is not so much a matter of distance as of detachment. At all costs, you must prevent your personality from turning back on itself, from building a citadel into which you will invite God only as a guest.

For when you want to pray, you must open your house and

bare your heart to God. Every way of life demands detachment. Married couples and those who are engaged to be married must become detached from self and open their hearts to each other; otherwise no love is possible but only a seeking of self in the other. At the very apex of love stands the love of God, which is a total and reciprocal gift of the lover to the beloved, of the one to the other. But, for us men, God is the Other, the other who will finally reveal Himself, in love, as the very source and mainstay of our being.

Before you can leave, you must do some hacking and slashing. As you cut the bonds that bind you, you will immediately become acutely and painfully aware that you are really cutting into yourself. But you don't have to wait until you are detached from everything and from yourself in order to start on your journey. You must make a start and, little by little, as you advance, the things that are dearest to you will fade away in the distance. There will be many things whose hold on you will be hard to shake off; that is only normal. If your heart is still attached to them, it will be sufficient to say to God: "I'm still clinging to such-and-such a thing, but I'm counting on you to set me free of it, so long as I'm going toward you."

What are you going to take along on your journey? Your whole self and nothing less. This may seem a strange answer, when we have just said that you must leave everything, particularly yourself. Yet it is true; you must carry your entire self with you. Many people only seem to set out on the journey to God. Instead of going themselves, they send a ghost, a kind of abstract model, in their place, while they put their real selves in safe keeping. They make a false, assumed personality, modeled on what they have read in pious books, and it is this artificial personality, this robot, this shadow of themselves that they send in search of God. They never really throw themselves, heart and soul, into the experience. It is not really they who set out on the expedition in search of God; they only send in their stead a sort of plaster saint, fashioned after the treatises on religious perfection that they have read. They do not go in person, but rather deputize an idealized double, a kind of *Doppelgänger,* to do the journey for them, and then they are surprised when all they get is disappointment.

When you are setting out, you must bring everything you possess—your body, your mind, and your soul: you must take the lot; your strengths and your weaknesses, your sinful past, your great hopes, and your basest and most violent urges. You must take everything, because everything must pass through fire. Every part of you must finally be integrated in order to make you a whole human being, capable of entering, body and soul, into the knowledge of God.

God wants to see standing before Him a real being, one that can weep and perhaps even cry out in agony at the searing, purifying effect of His grace; He wants a being that knows the price of human love and that is well aware of the attraction of the opposite sex. He wants to have a being that feels a violent desire to resist Him. And why does God want all this? Because He wants to see before Him a real human being and not a ghost, a straw man, in which there would be nothing for His grace to transform. Unfortunately, that is what happens frequently; only too many of those who "give themselves" to God offer Him merely a bogus personality for Him to act on. Hence it is not surprising that these people eventually come to see that they were made for something else.

However, the blame for this cannot always be placed on the shoulders of those who set out to seek for God but should be assigned to those who guide them. If the spiritual director insists on the formalistic aspects of piety and of the gift of self to God, he can hinder the soul from throwing its whole energy into the search for God. Instead, the soul fabricates a false image of itself in which God cannot find the power of life and action which He has put into His creation. If all we offer to God are plaster saints, He can do little with them except add some surface coloring.

When you have decided to set out and are all ready, body and soul, for the journey, you must put that body and soul into complete harmony with the Mystical Body of Christ, the

Church; you must live *with* the Church, feel the powerful rhythms that pulse through its liturgical life, its sacraments, its teachings and its constant care for souls. Then, as you live in harmony with the rhythm of the Church, you will find it easy to turn your whole being toward God and to live in the hope of soon feeling God's hand resting gently on your soul.

The end of the road is lost in God, and no one knows the road except Him who comes from God, that is, Jesus Christ. Therefore you must fix your eyes on Him alone, while still listening to the teachers whom you meet as you travel on. He is the Way, the Truth and the Life. He alone has walked that road as God and as man. You must put your hand in His and start your journey.

Chapter 3

When You Want to Pray

Anyone who wants to get close to God must set aside a short time each day to speak to Him alone, a time of intimacy and encounter with the Lord. In the same way, he must occasionally devote a longer period to penetrating more deeply into the discovery of that intimacy which is the expression of the love of God.

The actual place is of little importance provided the soul finds there sufficient peace and silence. It is true that faith can put us into contact with God at any moment of the day or night, but we must sometimes engage ourselves totally in prayer, and that is why we must, from time to time, turn aside from our normal occupations and plunge ourselves into prayer.

The place for prayer should be one in which the soul finds itself freest and in which the imagination and the intellect follow the soul most docilely in its search for God. This could be perhaps in one's home, in a church or chapel—it really doesn't matter provided that the soul can open itself out to God and gather together its usually wandering faculties. The soul must be there, completely attentive to God and not have its concentration shattered by noise, feelings, distractions, and silly thoughts. Christ Himself used to go aside to some quiet place among the hills or on the mountainside, bringing His disciples with Him.

Many people are prejudiced against such retirement from

everyday activity and the bustle of daily life. They think that such prayer is not made under real conditions and that, moreover, one should pray everywhere. It's true that we should pray everywhere; but those who speak like this and act accordingly run the risk of praying nowhere.

You must descend deep into yourself and into God in order that He may really show Himself to you in all your activities. You must dig deep to find wells that are abundant enough to irrigate your whole existence. The two dimensions, insight into God and self, are always complementary of each other. If all your actions are to become a prayer, you must have your soul in contact with Christ and with all of creation at a very deep level. Now it seems quite obvious that, in the normal conditions of life, this presupposes a momentary turning aside from the stream of human affairs in order to plunge into the deeper current that gives them life.

This is a form of prayer that community prayer cannot replace. Our Lord did say that when several people are gathered together in His name, He is in their midst. He Himself prayed with His disciples and had them take part in the sacred liturgy of His sacrifice. But He also went aside to pray alone, and He taught His disciples to do the same. The prayer of the Christian community has its full force only in the union between God, the Church and the Christians who make up that Church. If you forget that, you will fall into a formalism that would bestow on the community as such a sort of sacramental power. Now, just as it is Christ's sacramental and ecclesial presence that gives the community liturgy its depth, so also, due proportion being preserved, it is the depth of the union of souls with the Church and with God, with God in and through His Church, that gives value to community prayer.

It is difficult to keep a proper balance of appreciation between the respective values of community and solitary prayer. As a result of the pressures of modern life, many souls turn aside from a personal search for God. Yet the fate of each soul is decided between God and itself. It is to each individual soul that God puts the decisive questions: "Do you believe in Me? Do you love Me?"

Actually, there is no opposition between private prayer and community prayer, because both have God as their sole object. Their ways are different, for private prayer expresses itself in a different manner from community prayer, but these ways converge very quickly and both lead to God. Moreover. it is in solitude that the contemplative discovers his most intimate bond with his brothers, while community prayer should make him rediscover his personal relationship with God.

There is nothing shameful in feeling yourself drawn to solitary prayer, in following our Lord's advice to go into your room and close the door so that you can talk to your Father alone. You must enter the solitude of prayer with the conviction that, in finding God, you will find a greater love for your brothers; you are only going apart from them in order to find them better in God and in themselves. God draws those He loves into solitude until their souls are fully formed. Every man needs solitude to find and develop himself. Otherwise he will remain a child. He will be afraid of being left alone, face to face with himself. And if the Christian cannot live alone, face to face with his God, then the Church is only an immense herd and is no longer the Church of Christ.

That is why Christ, while He proclaimed His teaching in public, always tried to awaken in each individual soul faith in Him; and He promised the gift of His love and His presence in the soul as the reward of this acceptance of faith.

"When you want to pray, go into your room and close the door . . ." There you will find your God, and you will return to your brothers with your face shining with divine light.

Chapter 4

The Word and the Life

Sacred Scripture reveals to us the Word and life. Life is that mysterious, inexplicable force that animates everything that exists, the whole universe, mankind and all living creatures. In order to reveal this life and to give us access to it, we were given the Word. Christ, who is the Word and the Life, came to invite us to believe in the Word so that He might put us in closer contact with life. Life is for living and can find no other language but itself to express itself. That is why Christ invites us, not so much to understand life, as to experience it. "If only you recognized God's gift," our Lord said to the Samaritan woman, "and who it is that is asking you for a drink, you would have asked him instead and he would have given you living water" (Jn 4:10). The Word came to invite us to life. He described it for us, showed it to us, and made us understand it insofar as human language can make the reality comprehensible. But to the extent that man has not experienced life in himself, he cannot understand all that the Word wishes to reveal to him. Our religion is not primarily a religion of knowledge but one of life.

The divine life does not remain in God but goes out from Him with the gift that God makes of Himself. This life comes from God as a great river that supports and irrigates all human activity. This life nourishes all the cells of the spiritual organism, but no one can master it except Christ, who is both Life and Word. This divine life animates the Church, and the Church dispenses it throughout its whole liturgical body. The great mystery of the Christian life is this divine life that animates it. Christ possesses this divine life in its fullness because He is God, and He gives it to men, who receive it and make it their own insofar as their capacities permit them.

But this life remains like a great, mysterious river, unfathomable and boundless, so deep and so immense that man is as lost in it as the tiny fish is lost in the current of the sea that carries it along. It is a boundless flood that carries us in the great silence of its wholly divine immensity. Without Him who is both Word and Life, we would be always borne along without ever knowing what stream was sweeping us forward. But with Him, with Christ, the Incarnate Word, we receive light. In Him, life is expressed in a Word, which is also pronounced and manifested in the Gospels. Without this human Word, we would possess life but would not know whence it came or whither it was bringing us. Without the Word given to us in the Bible, we would be like so many men who feel the divine presence in them but who express it in language that is little more than the product of their imagination. This is the explanation for so many aberrations outside Christianity and unfortunately also within Christianity itself. Men heard Life itself speak, and their testimony leads us to its source. We can understand St. John's exultation as he wrote at the beginning of his first epistle: "This is what we proclaim to you: what was from the beginning, what we have heard, what we have seen with our eyes, what we have looked upon and our hands have touched—we speak of the word of life. (This life became visible; we have seen and bear witness to it, and we proclaim to you the eternal life that was present to the Father and became visible to us.) What we have seen and heard we proclaim in turn to you so that you may share life with us" (1 Jn 1:1-3).

The divine life has its own mysterious language which the words of Sacred Scripture explain to us; they show us the workings of grace in our souls. It is true that God shows Himself in a thousand ways, in nature and in our humanity. Often He shows Himself to the soul without any apparent relationship to the revelation which He made to the Jewish people and later to the whole world in Christ. But this does not invalidate the revelation made in the Incarnate Word without which human intelligence would be like the needle of a compass set spinning around by a magnetic field. Man's mind would no longer be able to understand and express the experience which it has had of God. That is why, in the history of the religious life, revelation in Christ remains the definitive pole that orients every other experience and every other partial revelation. Everything has been said to us in Christ because in Him God has given us everything that can be received by a creature, and the remainder is shown to us in the infinity of the divine mystery.

Anyone who wants to set out in search of God has a sure guide, one who is the Truth and the Life and the Way that leads thereto. No other spiritual guide is able or ever will be able to do more than point out the road or a part of the road, since, unlike Christ, no guide *is* the road from beginning to end. Yet, although human guides are only guides and nothing more, it is usually necessary to have one. Ordinarily, God does not wish those who are searching for Him to set out alone over the steep paths that lead to the depths of His mystery.

If you want to begin the search for God in contemplation, take up the Scriptures, study them under the direction of the Church, and choose a director who will keep you company on your journey. The words of Scripture, those of the Church and those of your spiritual director will be your light as you go in search of Life.

Chapter 5

The First Steps

You must enter into prayer with a broad view of God's omnipresence. The stage-setting for your prayer is not your room, nor is it the small, enclosed world of your personal thoughts, beautiful and wide-ranging as these thoughts can be, but can only be of the same dimensions as He whom you hope to meet, the dimensions of the universe, which is completely impregnated with God, which is from God and in God, "O God, your immensity fills the earth and the whole universe, but the universe itself cannot contain you, much less the earth and still less the world of my thoughts."

We are not speaking here of feeling the presence of God, and much less of picturing Him to ourselves. You can do that, but if you do, you risk being deceived by your own handiwork. God has never allowed Himself to be locked into a stage-setting. If you do form a picture of God, because it helps you, you must use it only as a mere point of application of the act of faith in the presence of God, since that is the essential act.

The divine revelation contained in the Sacred Scriptures has relegated the minor deities to oblivion. No longer are there household gods, gods in tall trees or great rocks. There is only one God, who is the God of the whole universe; in the new vision which the Scriptures have given to man, there is only one Lord of the universe in whom and by whom everything exists. "In him we live and move and have our being" (Acts

18:28). The act demanded of you at the beginning of prayer is the fundamental act of the human mind confronted with God, an act of faith in the omnipresence and omnipotence of God. Everything that is added to that act of faith to allow it to penetrate as deeply as possible into your psychological life is useful but in no way necessary. Some representation of God can help you to fix your mind and imagination in His presence, but you must not become attached to such representations, which can become a substitute for the act of faith and delude you into thinking that you have put yourself into the presence of God.

When you are praying, you may assume any posture you think fit; for example, standing when you are thinking about the presence of God, prostrating yourself to show your adoration, kneeling as a sign of humility, or even gazing around you to embrace the whole universe. In fact, this gazing around can perhaps be the clearest expression of your faith in God's presence in everything and in yourself, too. These postures and actions are quite easy; and undoubtedly you can think of many other suitable ones. The essential thing is to feel that you are really and actually standing before God and in Him.

To succeed in making an act of faith in God's presence, it is not necessary to exert superhuman efforts of concentration in order to empty your mind of every other thought and image that could encumber it. Ordinarily, this is impossible; and since it is impossible, it is not necessary. If your act of faith in the presence of God had to be at the level of thought, desire or vision, you would find it very difficult to make unless your mind were completely empty of everything else. But faith acts on another plane and is a much more profound experience. An act of faith can be made even in the midst of the worst distractions. People easily forget this, and it is understandable because it is hard to get a beginner to see that faith in God's presence can be exercised even though the mind cannot rest for even a moment in the consideration of His presence.

But you must not think that it is sufficient to make an act

of faith in God's presence and then let your imagination run riot and allow your mind to follow your imagination in all its wanderings. You really must make an effort to enter with all your heart into an active participation in the act of faith, which is the essential act. Since one thought is pushed out by another or even by some mental image, it is good to make use of very simple procedures. The thought that God is everywhere, in heaven, in the world of nature upon which you gaze, in the stars, in the firmament, in the power of the elements, the earth, the waters and the wind, in the power of life that is in every living creature—all these considerations will help you to replace the thoughts that cumber your mind with other thoughts that are in harmony with the act of faith which you are making. Hence you can just as easily form an image of God or of Christ in such a way as to fix your imagination. But you must not forget that all this is only on the psychological level and not yet on the level of prayer.

To achieve a peace of mind and heart that will permit your act of faith to expand and penetrate your whole psychological life, you can employ the simple means that regulate the rhythm of life. For example, if you simply say: "God! God! God!" slowly, in time with your breathing, you will quickly produce a soothing effect and will establish your soul in a peace that will make it responsive to the influences that come from God. Certain techniques, such as those of Yoga or Zen, can be used as aids to the act of faith, but only as aids, for, if you use them too much and for themselves alone, you may achieve a mastery of self, a peace, which may give you the illusion of union with God. However, such a peace, coming from the depths of one's being, can be nothing more than an apprehension of self in its deepest unity.

The danger is of remaining there and forgetting that if this natural contemplation does not open out onto God by faith, it can bring the soul to a halt before itself. Since the essence of Christian contemplation is the concentration of our whole being on God through faith, it is clear that purely natural methods of contemplation lose their importance in this context.

Chapter 6

From Meditation to Contemplation

Most treatises on the spiritual life recommend a form of prayer called "meditation" as being the most suitable for the beginner. The essence of meditation is reflection on truths of which the soul must be deeply convinced if it wishes to make progress in the love of God. The soul must first gain knowledge which will enable it to spread its wings in other forms of prayer, richer in content but less easily categorized. Methods of meditation teach the soul how to reflect on the truths of Christianity, examine them from all angles and connect them with each other in order to strengthen their power of convincing the mind.

Methods of meditation are a great help for souls who need to reflect, to weigh, to measure and to organize their faith. But only too often books on meditation are excessively "methodical" and full of closely reasoned, well organized and meticulously subdivided lists of "considerations." It is common knowledge that many souls go from point to point, from paragraph to paragraph, striving to extract the maximum profit from each idea as they conscientiously try to "put in" the time allotted to meditation. But the fact cannot be hidden that often too much method ties the soul down and stops it from making progress. Meditation is then no longer so much a means of finding God as an "exercise." Now, the object of meditation should never be the text itself, but rather the truth or the mystery which the text expresses, and, above all, it should be God, whom the truth expresses and whose inner life the mystery reveals.

The time of meditation ought to be a time of reflection in prayer, under the gaze of God. There should be no question of "studying" but of grasping the inner nature of the mysteries with the help of the divine light. For example, you can think over the various aspects of the mystery of the Holy Trinity and try to understand what the Persons are in their relationship with each other and with the Divine Nature. But such a reflection should be made in prayer, in a continuing act of faith that opens up the mind to the unknowable. The mystery of the Trinity can be understood only on the plane of faith, and it is therefore from this plane that God's light descends and must be received by our human faculties. In meditation, the mystery takes on a coherence that it did not have before being thus meditated on in this divine light. Now the divine life allows itself to be perceived by the mind, and it is this that gives meditation its true meaning. The mystery takes on a consistency which brings with it a testimony to the reality of the mystery.

Calm meditation on the mysteries in the light of faith will strengthen that faith by rendering the mind's acceptance of these mysteries more profound. Although the Holy Trinity will remain a mystery, this mystery will find in faith a coherence so luminous that the mind must necessarily accept it. The contradictions that a Moslem finds in the Christian teaching of One God in Three Persons will no longer cause any difficulty for one who meditates in faith. Even more, the mystery of the Trinity gives the key to all the fundamental problems of human destiny.

The Church took centuries to evolve a coherent expression of the scriptural references to the Trinity. Christ did not give the Apostles a scientific treatise on the question but simply allowed them, and us, to glimpse His place in the Trinity and His vital relationships with the other Persons. He revealed the inner life of the Trinity, and this was the light that made the formulation of the mystery possible; and it is by means of this formulation that the Christian soul can ascend to the very life of God. By examining the words of Christ and the teaching of the Church in the divine light, the soul places itself in the current of the divine life that comes from the Trinity and ascends toward the Trinity.

When you are meditating, you must not rest in your own thoughts but raise yourself at every moment to the plane of the divine thoughts. It matters little whether you read a book while allowing the thoughts it inspires to well up one after the other, or whether you meditate without using a book but by following the thread of thought suggested by the mystery you are meditating on. Whichever you do, the raw material of your meditation remains the same, namely, a series of words that speak to you about the mystery. You advance from thought to thought, but your mind is attentive, in an act of faith, to another train of thought that is being developed on the plane of faith. If you are reading, you are doing so on the two planes simultaneously with one glance, grasping the material in depth, savoring it and nourishing yourself on it. It is from the mysterious knowledge thus derived that your soul draws its strength, and you will soon be able to enter into greater intimacy with God.

The basis of meditation is a kind of "reasoned" contemplation, more regimented and structured than mystical contemplation. There is also a form of prayer which does not bring into play the faculty of reasoning or intellectual reflection to so great an extent, but rather uses man's ability to see, understand, sense and even touch spiritual realities. And this is already a form of contemplation. Sometimes the soul takes naturally to this form of prayer from the moment it begins to search for God and cannot pray in any other way. It does not need considerations, reflection or reasoning, but sees and tastes, and can act in no other way.

Other souls arrive at this point only after they have practiced meditation for a long time. A day comes when they no longer have any relish for the meditations that have nourished them up to this. Henceforth they are content to taste a truth, to savor it, and they can remain for days and even weeks completely taken up by the same mystery. They have now entered the way of contemplation and should be allowed to remain there and make progress in peace.

Chapter 7

The Mysteries in the Bible

In Christian prayer there is no effort on man's part that is not at the same time an acceptance of God's action. And this comes from the very nature of religious cognition, for the final goal of the contemplative's search is not a situation or a state but a union. Now, this union is a combined operation on the part of God and of man. That which will be a definitive union at the end of the Christian's journey is from the very beginning a joint effort of God and man.

In every Christian's search for God, activity is at the same time non-activity; effort is at the same time the suspension of effort in waiting upon the divine action. This simply means that there is a time for action and a time for non-action—action on man's part that is best expressed in non-action before God; non-action before God that is in the end the highest point of human activity.

When a person finds himself face to face with a mystery such as that of the Trinity, these stages of progress appear very clearly. He believes that God is One and Triune because of his faith in all that has been revealed about the Trinity. But when he tries to understand the mystery, he cannot really resolve the apparent contradiction of the terms. We must be under no illusion here: the distinction between the One Divine Nature and the Three Persons allows us to satisfy our minds, but this is not yet a real understanding of the mystery, a penetrating insight into the life of the Trinity.

The apparent contradictions at the level of our understanding can be resolved only in the divine light. That is why anyone who meditates on the mystery of the Trinity advances as far as he can with the aid of his native intelligence, but he goes forward with his eyes fixed on the very obscurity of the mystery, toward the place where God lives, as he waits for an interior light that will come to brighten the darkness that shrouds his mind. In the end, that light comes from God Himself.

When our Lady was visited by the angel of the Annunciation, she was taken aback by his greeting and particularly by what he had announced to her. She could see no solution to the problem because she "knew not man." She reflected on the question and then turned toward God to obtain light, which was immediately given to her. The answer was very simple. God raised her to another plane, and the Infant that was to be born of her would be conceived by the very power of God. Thus Mary was enabled to go beyond the surface appearance of the human situation and reach an understanding of the mystery of God's action. And it was God Himself who answered her humble enquiry.

That is what happens in every effort at contemplation in the face of the mysteries we find in Holy Scripture. God has spoken in ineffable words, and trying to understand these words at the level of expression is an exercise at which we can lose a lot of time. We must understand these words, not at the level of our psychology, but at the level upon which the realities which these words express are being and life, that is, in God.

It is not a question of giving the words of the Bible an allegorical sense, for thus you can delude yourself that you have understood something of the mysteries in Scripture. The most profound words in Scripture are those which reveal God Himself, a God who is not an image of man. That is why the real meaning of Scripture is God Himself... It is good to try to nourish yourself on the words of Scripture, but if you are looking there for nourishment that will satisfy you right away, you will perhaps find that that is nothing but a way to deceive yourself and to look for consolation, whereas God alone should be the object of your search.

The great danger is meditating on the texts of Scripture, mulling over them without paying much attention to the divine reality. And what is the result of these efforts? Nothing but words and feelings. You can, of course, derive some benefit from all this, but while you are getting this help you must not lose sight of the final knowledge, the knowledge that God alone can give and that is granted only to those who suspend their thoughts and activity in order to give their whole attention to God Himself.

Thus your mind ceases its efforts, and that is the best effort it could make, provided you have that great respect for God, who is life and light in your soul as He is elsewhere. The silence of your soul is a prayer, an awaiting, a desire for God and already a possession by Him.

If God showed Himself in a light or in words, people would pay attention to Him, but He ordinarily shows Himself only in an illumination of the power of faith. That is why so few have the courage to set out on this path. Nevertheless, it is the way of light, and everything we find in the Bible is an invitation to the act of faith . . .

The contemplative who thus engages in the search for the divine mystery is not advancing toward a problematic, far-off light, which he will reach only after years of effort, if at all. No, the illumination starts from the moment he takes up the Bible and turns the pages with the reverential attention of a child, who, with wide-eyed excitement, half expects the heroes to rise from the printed words of the book being read to him.

Christ does rise from the pages of the Bible, and the soul sees Him as the hunter glimpses the hind upon the hills, sees Him emerge from the mists of human knowledge into clear day.

Chapter 8

The Rhythm of the Bible

A very profitable exercise for those who are beginning the practice of contemplation is to take up a spiritual book, or, better still, the Scriptures, especially the Gospels or Epistles, and simply read, stopping from time to time to reflect and pray. Reading in this fashion is like walking through the world, holding God's hand.

First of all, you must allow the reality expressed in the sacred text to build itself up in your mind, because, as we have already said, meditation is not reflection on a text but attention to the action or reality expressed in the text. The words are only the expression willed by God of His personal reality or His action in the world.

Your faculties will react to the reading and form in you a representation of the reality which the text intends to convey to you. Your faculties build up, or better, *you* build up an intelligible representation of the hidden reality. But this representation, which should serve you as a foundation for an understanding of the mystery involved, can, in fact, turn into an obstacle, and it does so when it becomes the main object of your attention.

Because of this, a meditation that you thought very successful may have been a failure . . . because it created for itself an object that was easy to manipulate. Now, the Bible urges you to keep on destroying these "images" of the divine that you carve out to facilitate your spiritual life. You can smash these idols by a continual act of faith in the inexpressibility of the reality revealed. You seize avidly what God says to you about Himself, but once you express Him in terms that you can keep in reserve for savoring at leisure, you have nothing but dried husks, empty shells cast up on the beach when the tide goes out . . .

You open the Gospels and read the beginning of St. John's Gospel: "In the beginning was the Word; the Word was in God's presence, and the Word was God" (Jn 1:1). What wonderful things there are in these few words! You should read and reread this text slowly, giving the words their full meaning, going back again and again over the text with your mind fixed on the Word, the Light who enlightens you. The Word, the perfect expression of the Father, exists by the sole fact that the Father exists . . . and therefore He has always existed . . . This is perhaps too much for the human mind to grasp, but you are not asked to understand it; instead, you must reach that more profound knowledge that is attained at that point within you where your life is bound up with God's life.

The Jews and the Greeks had the Word and the *Logos;* and the Chinese have the *Tao*—the Way, the Word, the Principle of all things. By going over St. John's words again and again, our thoughts are projected beyond them, beyond all that our minds could grasp by themselves . . . and yet, by faith, by the light that comes to us from God and penetrates into the depths of our souls, these words take on meaning. It is not our minds that understand them, nor is it our inner heart that grasps them; instead, at that point within us where we derive from God, there awakens a knowledge that is inexpressible in human words. It is our deepest being that glimpses the mystery of God.

Your thoughts may wander for a while in subtle considerations, but this should be only for a while, because your mind must soon recollect itself *outside itself* by finding in God the bridgehead that it needs to set foot in the divine world.

The Sacred Scriptures are the unfolding of God's life in

human language. The revelation of the mystery is by no means presented as a riddle whose meaning is clear only to scholars or to the keenest minds. This would be the case if it were a question of understanding only the text. But it is God who must be understood, not only the text; and, all things considered, this is easier because it is possible for the simplest soul to outstrip the wise men on the road that leads to God. The words of Sacred Scripture can say much more to a simple soul than to a professional theologian because these words say what they have to say in the divine tones that the humble understand. In the Scriptures, you will find the truths and mysteries which Christ revealed in simple terms to His disciples, who were by no means theologians, but to whom He had given a sensitivity to God; and to have that sensitivity is to be a theologian.

The meditated reading about which we are speaking here is within everybody's capabilities. It does not demand the same effort as a meditation that is systematic, silent and without any concrete material for reflection. After all, the ideal is not to remain as long as possible without looking at a book or having distractions. This can be a useful exercise, but it can also be harmful to the soul.

The reading, meditated or contemplated, according to the passages selected, is the beginning of prayer and then its support and nourishment. It puts the soul in contact with God's action in this world. Hence it should not be centered on the study of biblical exegesis, which should have been done beforehand, if it is necessary. The text is the sign of God's presence and action, and therefore it is to the eyes of faith that God shows Himself in the text. From the beginning to the end of the Holy Scriptures, God appears at all the possible occasions of human life; and, in the end, the reader's deep attention gradually detaches itself from the text to focus on God.

Chapter 9

The Mysteries of Christ

Most souls are not at ease meditating on the great truths. They need something more concrete to think about, and they feel that only their intellects are at work in meditation. They want a form of contemplation in which they would be able to engage more fully and in a less abstract way.

God took this into account long ago and manifested Himself in a very concrete manner in all the phenomena that demonstrate to men that there are forces far superior to theirs. The fact that men may have interpreted as manifestations of God's omnipotence many phenomena that we can now explain by natural laws does not detract from the overall view. Everything comes from God, even that which can be explained by natural law.

God has always manifested Himself in the whole of nature, then more recently through the wise men and saints whom He chose to be His witnesses in the world, and finally He sent His Son, who is His Word. And everything this Son did during His earthly life was a manifestation of His divine being. Since He was able to express Himself and manifest the divine life in His words and actions, these words and actions are the best source material for the discovery of God.

In contemplating a scene from the Gospel, such as the Nativity, the soul feels itself more at ease than when confronted with a subject of meditation about God's redemptive plan. When meditating on the Nativity, you have the Redeemer

Himself there before your eyes, and everything that you see and understand speaks to you of God's love: "God's love was revealed in our midst in this way: he sent his only Son to the world . . ." (1 Jn 4:9). It is sufficient to be present in thought at the scene. There is no need to visualize every detail; as a matter of fact, doing so could be a hindrance. You must grasp enough of the scene to discover the inner mystery that it expresses and that animates it. As a result of your encounter with the Son of God in this Gospel scene, in His human condition, your mind will take flight toward the God who sent us His Son. You must be present at the scene, seeing, hearing, tasting and touching interiorly the nearness of God in this Child.

The act which allows us to seize God in this Child is in no way a marvellous feat of abstraction but an act of simple faith such as the one about which St. John speaks to us at the beginning of his first epistle, where he describes how he touched the Word of life in the human form of Christ. The infinite diversity of divine manifestations in a human life is sketched out in the life of Christ . . . and God continues to show Himself in our everyday life in a thousand guises.

In this way, you should go through Christ's whole life, living it again in company with His disciples and the crowds. Each person saw Christ in his own way, as the answer to his special problems or as an obstacle to his personal desires; and that is how each one judged Him. The contemplation of the mysteries of Christ is also our judgment, as Christ Himself said. We are given light; it is not imposed on us; and if we want to see more clearly, we can do so. But, in order to see clearly, we must go deep into His mysteries. When you enter a cave, you need a certain length of time to become accustomed to the darkness, and gradually you will observe that there is enough light to allow you to find your way. If you are afraid of taking the first step in the darkness, and refuse to do so, God's light will never illuminate your soul.

A great deal of imagination and feeling will enter into your contemplation of Christ's mysteries, but you ought not reject them, even if you are quite aware that they are not the essential elements of contemplation. Nevertheless, it may happen that you are taking too much pleasure in an idyllic representation of the Gospel . . . the shores of the Lake, the hills covered in spring flowers . . . Yes, our Lord did see all that and did enjoy it, but when He wanted someone to be His disciple, He looked him in the eye and told him: "If you want to follow me . . ." And the conditions under which His disciples had to follow Him were by no means those of an idyll on the flower-covered hills or the placid lake.

The essential element in any Gospel scene is not the setting, nor the actions, nor the words and much less your feelings, but Christ Himself. And this Christ must not be a figment of your mind, a projection of yourself. To avoid that danger, you must always contemplate the mysteries in total docility to the revelation that the Gospel gives us of Christ. None of the Gospels describes our Lord's external appearance, and no doubt the reason for this omission is to put us more directly in contact with the *Person* of Christ. Psychologists may have come to other conclusions, but we believe that knowing how Christ looked would have held us back on the road to the mystery of Christ Himself. We would have seen Him too clearly with the eyes of the body. St. Paul, who never met Christ, nevertheless saw Him and did so as really as all those who had been His disciples.

Beginners in meditation often complain that they have not got enough imagination; that is not important. The Gospel text provides the narrative of the events and is sufficient for the act of faith that reaches the very person of the Savior. If you do not reach Christ in this way by faith, you are only strolling through a lifeless waxworks when you are meditating on the Gospels. By the act of faith you attain the Word of God and you are given the divine life in abundance. It was by this act of faith that the woman who suffered from hemorrhages was cured, as so many others were cured and forgiven. And how many were there who, seeing the Son, saw the Father also? That is the crowning achievement of contemplation.

Chapter 10

The Mysteries and the Sacraments

In contemplation, the essential thing is always to put yourself into contact with grace by an act of faith in Christ. Meditating, praying or contemplating always involves immersing yourself in the current of divine life by an act of faith. Now, as you can see clearly from the Gospels, this act of faith needs the support of your intellect and your feelings if it is to take form in you. Insofar as it is a human act, the act of faith needs the same conditions as every human act if it is to reach maturity. We set out to follow Christ because of our first act of faith, and our progressive discovery of Him makes us deepen our acts of faith and renders them more expressive of our basic attitude. These acts engage us more and more according as we advance in the knowledge of Christ.

The world of the divine reveals itself only in the divinization of our souls, and trying to understand that world from outside is attempting the impossible. The whole universe is in God, because outside Him there is no possibility for anything whatever to exist. And this is even more true of man, who derives more closely from God than does the rest of creation. It is correct to say that we are in a divine environment, and this helps us to understand more clearly our relationship to God. But the word "in" can be misleading because it is meant here to express a relationship that is much more far-reaching, intimate, profound and essential than is indicated by its ordinary connotation. We use it here only as an easy way to help our minds to grasp the fact that God has given man a gift of His own being and existence. And the same must be said of St. Paul's use of the phrase, "in Christ Jesus."

Just as our relationship to God is not a matter of place, our relationship to Christ is not a matter of time. When we are contemplating the mysteries, their "where" and "when" are of little importance. It is, of course, good to know when and where a particular incident in the life of Christ took place. But the Evangelists were not too worried about the exact time and place of the incidents they recorded. Instead, they arranged their presentations of the life of Christ according to patterns that allowed them to show His thought, His life, and, above all, His very person to best effect. And since the important, the essential thing is this meeting of man with God in intimate communication, of which the Gospels give us so many examples, it matters little about the "where" and "when" of these examples. In this context, time hardly matters any more.

What does count, however, is to be present to a Christ who is Himself always present. When you are contemplating a scene from the Gospels, you like to put it into its proper setting because that helps you to fix your mind on it. You see it as past, as taking place in a certain period of history. Christ lived His earthly life, with all its mysteries, in Palestine, and, in that sense, those mysteries are in the past. But since they are acts done by Christ, who is risen from the dead and will die no more, they are always present and vibrant with life.

As Cardinal de Bérulle said, the mysteries of the Gospel are always "alive" in Christ. Therefore, when you are contemplating them, it is not enough to reconstitute them in their historical reality or even to relive them as you relive past events. In contemplating these mysteries, you must make yourself present to Christ, who communicates His life to you, by striving to share in the particular grace of the mystery you are meditating on.

The whole Chrisitan liturgy is built on the conviction that Christ is ever-living, and it allows us to participate in the graces of His mysteries according to a cycle which brings them into our lives, one after the other. At Christmas, the Church does not say "Christ was born two thousand years ago," but "Christ is born today!" At Easter, the Church tells us, "Christ is risen today." He triumphs over death *today*. Thus the eternal presence of the mysteries is shown to us as being parallel to the history of our own times.

You are united to each mystery by your act of adhering to it through faith, and this is a long way from a contemplation that is merely an effort of mind or a surge of feeling. You must not denigrate the efforts of any of your human faculties since they help you to give yourself totally to your act of contemplation, but you must understand clearly that your faculties merely express the profound act of your being as it searches for contact with its Lord.

What we have just said about contemplating the mysteries of the Gospel is carried out in the sacraments. A sacrament is, in fact, the act of Christ, the effect of which is expressed and made perceptible by the words and actions that form its structure. This is true of all the sacraments, but especially of the Eucharist, which gives us Christ Himself.

This is, we think, enough to show the internal continuity of the contemplative and the sacramental lives. Both of them are, as it were, slipways into the mighty current of divine life that flows down from God upon humanity and more particularly upon those who live in Christ. Prayer and contemplation are brought to perfection in the sacramental union. Every act of prayer is already a sign of that most intimate union which the grace of God accomplishes in the depths of the soul. It is even possible to discern the figures and outlines of the sacraments in the various forms of prayer. The important thing is to understand that the contemplation about which we are speaking has force and value only in the union with Christ for which it is preparing and which it brings about.

Chapter 11

When God Shows Himself

When the divine world opens up to him, man can do nothing but contemplate it in silence. Yet, in reality, he does not contemplate it, because it is still hidden to his eyes; but he feels it encompassing him on every side. This divine world is a presence that is felt everywhere, a power that acts in everything, and a life-giving sap that rises in the soul. Still, nothing is changed insofar as the outward appearance of things is concerned; everything in man's world continues to exist normally. Although there has been no change, the world takes on a new dimension, in its relationship of God.

Anyone who has had this experience is flooded with an unusual feeling of respect for the whole of Nature and for himself. It seems to him that he can touch the invisible, and feel the eternal. He goes through the world like a blind man who can see clearly, not, however, the world through which he is walking, but another world . . .

He did not arrive at this point in one leap. Little by little, he had begun to feel that long periods of reflection had no great meaning for him any more. One single thought was enough for him, one of those long thoughts that linger on the mysteries of the whole immense expanse of the faith. One single thought gave him more peace, more joy, than all his former "considerations"; and this thought never became oppressive because it was centered on the divine mystery and not on itself.

This simplicity is soon reached in every form of prayer that the contemplative uses. He can remain for a long time with his mind fixed on one Gospel scene. He sees Christ, but his vision has nothing to do with imagination; he sees Him with a perceptiveness that is not a mere gaze; instead, he seizes Christ with all his soul. This very special way of seeing is the result, the flowering, of a long-standing habit of contemplation which has sharpened the contemplative's ability to see with all his soul, and God then shows Himself to him.

At this point in the development of the contemplative life, one's human acts have a very great simplicity and unity. The discursive process of thought and the multiplicity of feelings have given place to acts which are very simple but very intense and which involve one's whole being.

In the evolution of contemplation there is obviously a development that is analogous to the simplification and unification of human thought. Although it is possible for a contemplative to attain a prayer of very great simplicity, he will never be able, solely by his own intellectual efforts, to attain this simplicity of action to which man is led when God shows Himself to him. Although this manifestation of God is very mysterious and hidden, it produces, as a necessary consequence, the concentration and deepening that places man in a state of pure attention to God.

Contemplating God cannot be a merely human act, because God is not something that man, by his own unaided efforts, can ultimately succeed in perceiving. He is an object of vision for us in somewhat the same way as are the stars, which we see by their own light. We see God by the light that He sends us, and, even more, He is the power in us that makes us capable of seeing Him. If a man consents to be the human agent of the divine action, he will see God in His own light.

God endows human actions with an astonishing power which

is perceptible only to faith and which man discovers when he sees God; and when he does see God, he understands that he does so only by the power of God. When the contemplative looks into the depths of his own soul, he sees mounting within him feelings which can be explained by the ordinary laws of psychology and which are formed, just as other feelings are, in the depths of the unconscious.

Nevertheless, in seeing God, the contemplative discovers a new dimension in his soul. He understands that the faith that prompts his feelings comes from a much more profound source than the unconscious. In the highest act of contemplation, man discovers his true depth, which is divine because it is a relationship to God. This is clearly what St. John meant when he wrote: "We shall be like him, for we shall see him as he is" (1 Jn 3:2). We shall be like Him in our humanity, and this resemblance to God in our humanity is the true depth of the human soul.

At this stage of contemplation, the divine world is still a very mysterious one. Man has only a simple, overall perception of it. It is still an indistinct universe, one in which God seems to remain inactive. That is why the contemplative finds that he is drawn to a deep recollection. He no longer ventures to make very definite acts of prayer; in fact, he is no longer able to make such acts. He is in that divine world, in the presence of the God who dwells in it and animates it. Divine grace enlightens him interiorly, but with a very unobtrusive light. A profound harmony exists between the soul and God, but this harmony finds it difficult to express itself except by a basic docility.

Many contemplatives never go beyond this stage, which then becomes a permanent state and which assures the soul that it possesses the essential element of contemplation, that is to say, contact with the God of all things, beyond words and feelings. At certain moments of more intense recollection, however, such contemplatives may perceive the presence of God more strongly and in a more definite way.

When a contemplative has this experience of God for the

first time, he may feel that he has arrived at his destination. However, more often than not, he has a presentiment that a new world is about to open up to him, but that, before he can take another step forward, his inmost being must be freed from its too-human bonds. And therefore he stands in simple silence before God, waiting for Him to free him and open the door to him.

Chapter 12

The Imperceptible Gleam

At this point in his journey, the contemplative sees his own world in balance with the divine world that is beginning to show itself to him. Until now, he knew that divine world only through faith, but now he is beginning to be aware of it in all its mystery. The perception that he now has of the divine world is strong enough to balance against his human world. That is why he lives in a state of expectation, with one foot on the threshold of the divine world which he knows he has been invited to enter. Voices come to him from inside, but he remains on the threshold, waiting for the invitation to enter, standing in silence at the meeting point of the two worlds.

At this threshold, the soul is filled with an extraordinary presentiment. It knows that it will enter some day. It is not uneasy, because the mere fact of having arrived at the threshold is already such a great grace that the soul could remain there for years to come and still be content.

While human action and divine action seem to be in a harmonious balance on this threshold, the situation will change once the contemplation has crossed the threshold into the divine world. Then God will take over and will introduce the soul in His house, leading it, guiding it and acting toward it in His own divine way. The divine action will not longer manifest itself in the secret recesses of the soul but will do so openly. The soul's invisible Companion on the long journey through the night will reveal Himself as a great friend who treats the soul with the generosity of a prince, the affection of a friend and the love of a spouse.

All this begins in greatly varying ways for different souls. After months and perhaps years of an obscure presentiment, one day the soul, while looking at a landscape, or during a meditation, or in the middle of practically any task, perceives a presence, within or outside itself, in the landscape, or in whatever place it may happen to be at the moment. This presence allows itself to be felt as an inaudible summons, a very gentle voice, a love which comes from afar and which invites the soul to love in return. It is a pinpoint of starlight in the sky, a glimmer of light in the darkness, a song without words, a silent invitation. But it can also be an elusive atmosphere that envelops all things, a new imperceptible dimension to everything that exists.

The contemplative who had never before found anything unusual in his prayers can now only be silent. He waits, saying nothing, straining his ears, hardly daring to breathe, and suspending all his intellectual powers, as he watches for a word, a gesture, any kind of signal that may come from that mysterious world which has just arisen out of his familiar universe. Every thought is stilled in him. And this may be all that happens this first time. He may feel no other effects. But his soul can no longer shut itself up within itself to savor its own thoughts. It waits for a word, a look, from Him whose presence it has discovered and whose call it has heard.

No matter how feeble this perception of the divine presence may be, it is a rent in the veil that hid from the soul the presence of God found in all things. A long time must still pass before this presence will show itself in all its splendor and immensity. But the soul is filled with what it has seen of God, and, from this point on, its prayer and its life are changed. It knows that God is there, that He is everywhere. Hitherto, it had known this without perceiving it, but now that it does perceive it, it knows it with a knowledge that is full-flavored.

In the great entrance hall just beyond the threshold which the soul has crossed, it hears sounds coming from within the house itself. Already it has an idea of the immensity of the house from the sound of the voices coming from it. It has entered into a new mode of thought and feeling. It left at the door all the beautiful reflections that used to sustain it in its prayers, for it no longer needs them . . .

It feels peace, joy, and a calm love. In addition, everything is so simple, so transparent, it seems almost unreal compared with the good clear thoughts it used to have. But this transparency is only a reflection of the divine presence that is manifesting itself. This presence is imposing on the soul its own mode of thinking and perceiving. God's transparence renders the soul transparent, too, and makes it feel as light as a feather in this world of human dullness.

If God allows Himself to be perceived just a little more strongly, the soul will find itself in a state of repose and self-abandonment, and completely caught up in divine peace. This is known as the prayer of quiet. It is not an ordinary state of rest for the human faculties. The soul is now, as it were, emptied of all its passions, desires, ambitions, and even its thoughts. It is carried aloft into the divine presence, as the morning mist is drawn up by the rising sun. In fact, this is the repose of the soul in love, in a requited love.

Ordinarily, these first manifestations of God are transitory. God makes Himself perceived by the soul, and then everything goes back to normal. Things return to their dimensions as creatures. But the faith that has penetrated the mystery of God's presence in all things can no longer have the same outlook on the world as it had before. Often it seems to the soul that God has retired into His creation but has left behind in the world an almost imperceptible gleam of His light that remains for the soul as a reminder of His divine presence.

The soul should not try to reconstruct from memory the presence that has vanished. If it tries to do so, it will only succeed in deceiving itself by nurturing a spurious feeling of God's presence on its memories of the grace it has received in the past. Instead, it should wait for the return of Him who is just as close now as He was when His presence was felt, by living in the firm belief that God's love remains even when He Himself seems to have gone.

Chapter 13

The Night in the Desert

God allows Himself to be perceived and sometimes even touched, but He remains the Unknowable, the Unreachable. The soul knows that He is there, and cannot doubt that He is. Nevertheless, if it tries to approach Him to get a closer view, to reach Him, to touch Him, it finds nothing but a thorny bush on which it wounds itself. This is the mystery of those familiar objects that serve as raw material for the revealing of God. In the desert, the bush burned but was not consumed. The flame was more in Moses' soul than in the bush.

God is not His perceived presence or the burning flame, for nothing can express Him perfectly. He is never what I see, never what I touch. But I see Him in what I see, and touch Him in what I touch. My faith illumined by divine grace touches Him and sees Him, and this contact is real, as are my seeing Him and my meeting Him. I cannot doubt that. God does everything in such a way that I cannot doubt it. Perhaps I shall doubt it later on, but how can I doubt it now?

God is always beyond what He shows of Himself. No matter how lofty one's mystical knowledge may be, this is always the case, and if the soul forgets it, it will attch itself to what it knows about God. It wants to take possession of Him, as of something permanently acquired. This is only an illusion. How many people have wasted their time in clutching at shadows, at the signs of God's presence to which the soul becomes attached rather than to God Himself!

God remains far beyond all perception and all human reach. The God whom I can name is not God at all; the God whom I can grasp is not the true God. God is never grasped while He pauses in mid-flight. He is like a comet that streaks across the sky and never stops. Knowledge of God is a perpetual movement, one that never ends; and here especially, the concept of "never" contains the secret of "always." And it will be thus even in the Beatific Vision. Then our souls will no longer be weighed down with the heaviness of earth, but will advance in the discovery of God with the infinite speed of the revelation of divine love. Our rest will consist only in this infinite movement of discovery of the divine mystery. This will be for us the great light of Heaven.

For us now, every manifestation of God carries within it evidence that He is still more than we see. The greatest lights are, at the same time, the discovery of the Unknowable. Darkness shows up in the light, and the light is shown to be darkness. In this life, the more the soul grasps God, the more it discovers, by means of the light He gives it, that He is still farther off. At the beginning, the soul thought that it could give Him a name. But the more it advances, the more the names it can give Him become empty of meaning, and the very signs of His presence become an obstacle to His being more profoundly present. And that is the way it happens with all knowledge of God in this life; the great light that falls upon the sands of the desert is deepest darkness.

In the light with which He enlightens the soul, God reveals Himself as unknowable. The light that used to enchant the soul becomes darkness. The presence in which God used to give Himself becomes His absence. The soul advances over the trackless desert in the dark of night. The sinner does not feel God's absence. Only he who is already living in great intimacy with Him knows the night and the desert about which we are speaking. Mystical authors speak about two nights, the night of the senses and the night of the soul, but only the latter is the real mystical night.

Sometimes the soul finds itself buried in a dark pit, with no light and no means of escape; or it may come up against a towering wall of darkness and silence, with no way around and not a glimmer of light. What one soul feels is a desert, another soul will experience as a night.

Sometimes the night is so dark, the desert so empty, that the soul despairs of ever finding the joy of God's presence. But it should not become anxious. God will return. Actually, He does not have to return, because He is already there. And it is because He *is* there that the soul finds itself in darkness in the middle of the desert. This night and this desert are the obverse of God, as the confused tangle of threads is the obverse of a tapestry. The desert and the night are not therefore simply trials to be borne but are already ways of knowing God; they are the discovery of the Unknowable by a new manner of knowing.

In the night and the desert, God detaches the soul from the ordinary ways of perceiving the spiritual. He detaches it from all that can be perceived by the senses, from its spiritual consolations and from partial knowledge. He refines in it the faith that alone is capable of penetrating His mystery. He divinizes its being and its modes of spiritual action.

The soul thinks that it is immobilized, imprisoned at the bottom of its pit, stopped short at the foot of the immense cliff that it cannot climb. In fact, in the silence of this night, God is carrying it along and helping it to ascend the gigantic foothills of the divine world. Without the soul's being aware of it, God is making it capable of reaching out to and penetrating His mystery.

The soul cannot see anything because it is travelling in a world to which its eyes have not yet become adapted. It feels so alone because God's presence is quite different from a human presence. God is so "other" that He can be seen only by His own light and can be loved only with His own love.

That is why the ways of contemplation are so heartbreaking in those religions that do not know this light or this love.

The soul should not lose courage, for it is through God's absence that it draws near to Him, and it is in darkness that it discovers Him. In reality, God is so close to the soul that, if He showed Himself to it, it would be astonished to see that He is so near.

Chapter 14

God Comes into the Desert and the Night

This period in the desert and the night lasts for a more or less extended time for different souls. The more docile a soul is to the Lord, the more likely it is to pass quickly through these trials. But only God knows what He is asking from each soul, and His ways of acting are always very mysterious.

When the soul is in the night, it feels such a distaste for all things, for itself and everyone else, and even for prayer, that it is plunged into great suffering. It would like to be able to find its former peace, but it cannot fashion happiness for itself out of the memories of the past. If it did, it would be unfaithful to God, who wishes it now to suffer this solitary and painful night.

The happy hours of blissful quiet that it used to know have left it with a profound nostalgia. It looks back to the past with empty eyes, while the present has nothing to offer it but solitude and loathing. All it can do is try to derive some encouragement from remembering past graces, and from hope in the future. But even the future seems closed to it . . .

It must not try to escape from its night of suffering, for then it would lose all the benefit thereof and would no longer be compelled to pierce the darkness with the eyes of faith. For faith, there is no night; but the light that faith gives the soul is hard and cold. The soul yearns to regain the warmth of its former joy and love. But its God is no longer there to enlighten it, console it, and help it pierce His mystery with a penetrating glance. Who can hear it, now that its voice is lost in an immense silence? Now there is nothing but an icy silence in the dark night. Those who have never undergone this trial cannot know what it is. The soul can cry out to God, over and over again, but it has to become aware of the fact that its voice is being lost in the void; yet God does hear it.

God is waiting until the soul has accepted its night and its desert, until it lives there completely, without thinking about the joys of the past and without sighing after anything but Him, its Lord. The soul must be emptied of itself on to the sand or stony soil of the desert. It must give up all its human desires and be emptied of them. It must be able to utter only one cry: "God, God, God . . ." unendingly.

When its whole being is nothing but a desire for God, when it is nothing but a sigh to God, then He loves it and is prepared to show it the immensity of His love. For the soul now, the world is dead and so is life; nothing is alive in them any longer but the only living One, the Lord God.

In the night in the desert, the Lord is present in a manner so mysterious that the soul is scarcely conscious of Him. It can neither advance nor retreat, but plunges deep into itself with dizzying speed. It strips itself of everything that is peripheral to it and becomes, in God's presence, a mere creature, fully and acutely conscious of its complete dependence on Him.

It knows that God is working in it, but He does so at such a depth that the soul cannot reach there. Sitting all day beside the unfathomable abyss that has been hollowed out in it, it waits for the visit of Him who has reduced it to this extremity.

Sometimes He does come. Suddenly, He appears as a great light in the soul, as a dazzling beam that shoots out of the night and lights up the desert. During these divine visitations, the soul often has time only to utter a cry, one cry which signals both the arrival and the departure of Him who is passing by.

But this light is so bright that it is worth more than all the consolations of the past. In a soul stripped of self, detached from every spiritual joy, reduced to being merely itself and nothing more before God, the divine light flashes on it and on God. One flash is enough. The atmosphere of the soul is so pure that there is nothing in it that can act as an obstacle to the light. In one glance, it sees and understands everything: God, itself and the whole world; it sees them in their immensity and also in that inexplicable bond of their meeting in the inmost depths of the soul.

The light shoots out from everywhere at once—from the soul, from the world and from God. It lights up everything at once, from one horizon to the other, from the depths of the being of all things to the inner recesses of God's being. The soul has had time only to let out a cry in response to God's coming, a cry into which it puts its whole being. Never, in the consoling quiet that it used to experience, did it even suspect the existence of this depth of things and of God. It has seen all this in the one flash of light from God. It has seen, but now everything has finished, and the night has once more fallen on the desert.

The soul looks at itself in the night and sees that a light is coming from it, one that it did not suspect existed, that sprang up as God passed by. And this light will not fade. God has passed in the night, and the night is forever illumined. But this light has a very special clarity, the clarity of the divine mystery in the night of faith—that is the only way to describe it. Indeed, it cannot be properly described, nor is it necessary to try, since those who have seen it will understand.

The Lord has passed by, and His light has enkindled a great light in the soul. The desert is still a desert, and the night remains a night, but the soul has seen its God and cannot forget Him. Never again will its desert be simply a desert, or its night be as black as ebony.

Chapter 15

The Divine Presence

After some months, or perhaps not until several years have passed, the night will become less dark and the desert less arid. God's visitations will be more frequent, and He will no longer come like a flash of lightning, only to disappear again as quickly over the far horizon. The whole desert will blossom with His presence, at first like an almost imperceptible spring, but later like a radiant summer.

The soul feels that it is entering another world. Its solitude is no longer solitude, and it sees everywhere Him whom it loves and who has hidden Himself for so long. Now He seems to appear in all places and at any moment; He shows Himself in the most arid corners of the desert and in the darkest caverns of the night.

The desert and the night now seem completely impregnated with the divine presence; the night has become luminous with it, and the desert is inhabited with this total presence. Everything exists and moves in this presence. More spacious than the broad horizon, it spreads in all directions; deeper than the abysses of the earth, it vivifies that earth down to its most secret center. Greater than the earth, vaster than the heavens and even than the entire universe, it is still more tenuous to the touch than the impalpable morning mist. The largest of created things do not hide it or obscure it any more than do the most imperceptible ones. In this presence and by it, the mind plunges to the innermost depths of all things. With a single glance, the soul sees everything that exists and also the divine presence that is in all things and in which all things are found. With a single glance, the soul sees everything at two depths of being, that of concrete existence and that of existence in God.

Whether I open my eyes or close them, this divine presence is always there. It does not vanish when I close my eyes, nor does it hide itself when I open them. It is there, in the night and in the light. It is a continual presence that extends from the depths of my being to the outermost limits of the universe and as far as God. It is the unity of all things, the power that maintains them in existence.

Although this presence is everywhere, the soul perceives it in its own depths, as an imperceptible point, a point in which the power that is spread throughout the universe is found concentrated at the boundaries of the created and the eternal. In this point all the divine power is gathered; it is a point without any dimension other than the meeting of the divine and the created.

It also happens sometimes that the soul which has experienced the divine presence in all its immensity, sees it gradually compress itself into that imperceptible point. It seems to the soul that the whole presence of God, which suffuses the whole universe and the soul itself, has become so concentrated that it appears to be returning to its Source. This point can become so tenuous and imperceptible that the soul can grasp it only by an act of faith. The soul will remain in the silence of adoration before that which lies beyond the perceived presence of God, namely, before God Himself.

In this experience of the divine presence, the soul understands how this presence comes from God and goes back to Him. It also understands how all things are in God and how He is in all things, especially in itself, in its deepest recesses. The immensity of the divine presence in the entire universe is not vaster or more profound than the presence at the bottom of the soul. It is not a lifeless presence but a vibrant one, that animates everything. It is a loving presence that brings to the soul all the fatherly solicitude of God for souls and for the world.

This presence is sometimes so strong that the soul sees itself plunged into an ocean of life that bears it away. It is penetrated and impregnated by it, as is everything around it.

All the power working in the universe is expressed in this presence which seems so gentle and simple that one is inclined to ask where its strength is. Yet it was this strength that launched the world into existence and that has kept it in existence since then. This is not, therefore, a product of imagination but perception of the divine power in the universe, the power of creation and the power of grace. The mystic does not invent what he sees, but simply sees things at a greater depth than other people. He is able to grasp how everything is sustained in God and animated by Him; he sees how souls live with the very life of God.

For the mystic, the divine presence is the presence of grace. His spiritual faculties, his soul, appear to him to be penetrated and animated by this presence. He lives in God; he lives by God. In everything—in his daily life, in his prayer, in the sacraments—he sees the divine power at work in the presence that manifests itself.

After his long sojourns in the desert and the night, this continual presence of God is a real paradise for the mystic. May he retain it always! But if it seems to be slipping away from him, he should pursue it in God by faith; and may he remain attached to its Source!

Chapter 16

Discovering the Depths of the Soul

By showing Himself in the soul, God has lighted up its depths and has awakened in it new capacities for seeing and understanding. The contemplative discovers the reality of the soul and, in it, intimate manifestations of God. By a new mode of knowledge, he discovers God's presence within him, and soon he will perceive God's action in him in an almost immediate and direct way. The man who is accustomed to living in the world of sense and ideas cannot understand what this new mode of knowledge is, but both Christian and non-Christian mystics are agreed that he perceives God's action in him.

The first effect of the manifestation of God's presence in the soul is that it discovers itself and becomes conscious of its own existence. This exploration of the soul by itself, of which psychoanalysis uncovers only a few scraps, is made possible by spiritual insight. In manifesting itself, the divine light illuminates the whole area around its focal point. At the beginning, God's presence is still very obscure, and the soul has great difficulty in perceiving itself, but according as that presence becomes more perceptible, the soul sees that it can both receive God's action and act by itself.

In the divine light, the soul suddenly sees itself as a limitless universe that seems to extend to the very dimensions of the God who is showing Himself to it, and as a center of unbreakable unity in its personality. In its contact with the world of sense, it can easily see itself as a mere center of convergence for sense impressions, but, when it discovers God's oneness in itself, it understands that it is the indefinable center in which are based the unity that it receives from God and the multiplicity that it receives from the sense. It is the point of convergence for everything that exists. Depending upon which of these two aspects, unity or multiplicity, it is viewing, it can think that it is the Absolute, as in Hinduism, or simply the reflection of an illusory world, as in Buddhism. In discovering God, it discovers its true unity and its role as the great gathering point, in consciousness, of all creation.

When the presence of God enters the soul, it first sees itself as being inhabited by the presence and then completely taken over by it, as if it were *all* presence to an even greater depth within it. Plunged in divine grace and completely filled with that grace, it sees itself as one beloved by God. In this grace, it finds that it is more "centered," more "one."

As we have just said, the divine presence lights up the depths of the soul by showing itself in the soul, which then knows itself and God in one and the same light. The "closer" the "area" in which the divine light shows itself is to the source of that light, the more deeply the soul sees into itself. It can thus follow the rays of light upwards and ascend to attain God. Oh, it cannot reach Him, but sometimes, by means of a very special illumination from Him, it can find itself so close to Him that it has touched Him.

Happy the soul whom God has drawn so close to Him that it can say: "I have seen God!" It says that it has seen God. We must understand exactly what that means, because there is no question here of ordinary seeing. Instead, in showing Himself, God allows Himself to be perceived by the soul, and for that purpose He gives it senses that are capable of receiving His light. It is difficult to explain how this perfecting of the natural senses is brought about. Besides, these are the senses of the mind—the mind's hearing, the mind's sight—which becomes capable of apprehending God.

God's presence in all things is a hard fact. The question is whether that presence can become recognized as the divine presence. A little reflection on the very makeup of creation, which God did not simply form and then leave aside, will show us how that creation, for a mind enlightened by God, can become a sign of His presence. If we admit the reality of God's showing Himself in the humanity of Him whom we call Christ, there is no further problem. The knowledge about which we are speaking is of the same order: in Christ, the human and the divine blend perfectly together.

God has marked all of creation with the sign of His presence, and He has given the person who has sought Him for so long in meditation a new sense that renders him sensitive to the signs of His presence and His action. Often the soul really sees only in the light of faith, but it can happen that God's presence manifests itself so strongly and so clearly that the soul can say: "I see."

There are many degrees between the initial shock that surprises the contemplative—it is a surprise because its impact is both penetrating and silent—and the full illumination of God's presence. The soul advances from one light to another, as it traverses broad zones of darkness and desert. It progresses and discovers itself as it discovers God. One of the most astounding things in the mystical life is this progressive discovery of God, which one day becomes total illumination. So many mystics have longed for it, but have never attained it! Of all the roads to God, the one that passes through Christ is the most direct and leads furthest, beyond all created things and to the very heart of God.

Chapter 17

When God Shows His Love

Many souls attain an habitual perception of God's presence in themselves and in all things, both in the repose of prayer and in the midst of activity. In this constant apprehension of God's presence, they find an astonishing peace, yet at the same time they feel the demanding nature of this presence. They can no longer taste the peace that certain souls derive from withdrawing into themselves; they cannot live a selfish life, because God's presence opens them up to Him, the world and everything that exists. But they are in danger of finding His presence completely natural because it is so much an integral part of creation.

Now God calls the soul to Him in an intimacy that is more ardent and that demands a more total response from it. The calm, untroubled presence that the soul used to enjoy in peace now reveals itself as an active power. God is no longer this presence diffused throughout Nature and in which the soul remained silent; rather, He is the great Being who gives existence and life to all creation. This calm power of God's initial presence begins to bestir itself in somewhat the same way as the surface of the sea does when the wind gets up and the waves rise higher and higher. This presence was only the first approach of a Being who wants an answer to every word and an act in response to each of His own actions.

From this presence there springs a restrained power that suddenly awakes. God acts in the soul, animating it and bringing pressure to bear on it. Soon He makes it feel the omnipotence of His purifying action by infusing into it a grace that lifts it up and transforms it. The soul feels growing in it a life that seems to it like a participation in God's own life. It sees how the life that is in it flows from the Trinity, as water from a wellspring. This life which is much deeper, more ample, stronger, and more ardent than its own, comes from God and takes it over like a formidable force which it cannot resist. Its own life explodes into the life of God. It is borne along like a swimmer caught in a current and tossed about by the waves. Although it is in the grip of the great movement of God's life, it is not lost in it; it is being swept along by the tide but it emerges on the crest of a wave. The movement of the divine ocean carries it, penetrates, flows over and encloses it; and, in this great movement that it cannot control, it feels itself called to say "yes!" to the wave that is bearing it forward to the ocean into which it is plunged, for the ocean is God, and the wave is His life.

God thus shows Himself in man's life as the most profound, most intense, most immense and most total force, the definitive power. He also shows Himself as the perpetual Creator of all things. He is not a tranquil, sleeping force in created things, but is the formidable power from which all power derives its strength and impetus. The soul would be terrified if it saw the abysses of God's power. Sometimes it glimpses them, and the universe opens up before it, allowing it to see God as the foundation of all things. But ordinarily it sees Him working in the created things around it and, above all, in itself.

God is not particularly interested in demonstrating His power. Instead, He wishes to show the love which, on the very first day of creation and ever afterwards, led Him to put this world into existence. All of that, all the manifestation of formidable strength involved in bringing the world into existence, is the fruit of an act of love, an act of love toward something which did not exist until He created it. And now we must clearly understand that God shows Himself thus in action, not as a display of strength, but because the whole world is in fact built on an act of love, one that is to be perfected in the union of God with man. On God's part, the act of love is always perfect, and He has performed this act from eternity. But He comes now to prepare the soul by His presence, to habituate it to Him, and then, when the soul is sufficiently aroused, He shows Himself as a Being full of life. He shows Himself to the soul as a partner in the only true love, that is, total love, the love that is the reciprocal gift of two beings, one to the other.

God really wishes to share His glory, but He cannot do it apart from love. That is why He does not display His greatness but shows His desire to be received by the soul and to receive it in the same act. Is not this the perfect act of love? He does not offer the soul the chance to live off His riches or at His expense. Rich and powerful though He is, He offers His inmost life to the soul, a life which the soul can receive by opening up its own life to it. The soul sees that it is completely penetrated by God's action; nevertheless, this divine life does not crush it. There is no longer any need for that; the time of hard trials is past. But the time of tranquil peace has passed also, and now is the period of fruition, the union of the soul with God.

The graces of love and knowledge are stronger here than during the period of God's simple presence. The soul sees that its life is God's life. This is no longer a simple presence, strong as that presence might have been; it is true union, the union of love that cannot be described. God shows Himself and acts in the soul, and gives His love in the gift of His own life. The soul, completely caught up therein, receives from God and renders back to Him all that it has received from Him by detaching itself from itself, and this is the union of love.

Chapter 18

Divine Lights and Graces

In order to show the stages in the discovery of God, we have explained first how the soul becomes conscious of His presence, and then how it is caught up in the manifestation of His transforming action. But the manifestations of God can be of a thousand different kinds because, for each soul, God is its own God and never simply everybody's God.

In the history of a soul, we must discern the essential axis of its evolution. This history obeys laws that are unvarying enough to enable us to consider them as generally applicable. This is the line of development that we have tried to present, simplifying it, however, to make it clearer.

And then, in addition, there is the multitude of different ways in which grace is manifested to individual souls. Often these graces are, in the firmament of the soul, like meteors that can distract it from what is essential. Those lights, tastes, intuitions and very deep feelings make a greater impression on the soul than the essential continuity of God's action. They are more brilliant and more violent, and the soul is sometimes transported out of itself by them, experiencing moments of ineffable joy. But it must understand that these lights and graces are only the expression of the work that God is doing within it. A sudden glimpse of the divine mystery in the unimaginable clarity of an intuition that lasts for a shorter time than the most rapid thoughts, is, at the same time, the manifestation of a transformation of the soul in God. We must understand clearly that these graces are the blossoming in one's consciousness of God's action in the soul, for it is in the soul that He acts with the greatest freedom.

In the soul's evolution there are decisive moments. For example, the soul may enter a deeper contemplation as a result of the sudden, piercing sight of God's grandeur or of His love or His unfathomable mystery. It can know Him in that emptiness that is void of all possible knowledge, in which it simply stands, without a word to say, without even a thought, completely gripped by the impossible mystery.

It can happen that a soul will suddenly discover that "God is there," that He "is," since both are the same thing. At the same time, it will see itself in the concrete universe, the real world, upon which it stands, and also in God. God can give such graces to a soul even before it so much as dreams of setting out on the path of prayer; and these graces may determine the whole course of a life or the conversion of a sinner.

These graces and lights are not independent events in the life of the soul but point out and reveal its inner progress. That is why they are very important and why they must not be regarded as secondary, inconsequential manifestations. These are the glowing flowers of a garden whose soil is very rich. They reveal the mystery of God's action, and the soul simply must not allow itself to be captivated by the brilliant color of the flowers or intoxicated by the heady scent of their perfume. God alone counts.

When the soul is in the night, God may visit it with disconcerting suddenness. Convinced that it is quite alone in the desert, it does not expect to come face to face with someone at a bend in the path. And yet that is what happens. God descends upon the soul with lightning swiftness and wounds it with a shaft of light or an arrow of love. These manifestations seems utterly out of place in the desert, yet the soul should see in them the proof of God's love and action. A work is being performed in the soul at such a depth that the soul cannot perceive it. These descents of God make it conscious of this work and are meant to renew its courage and make it resolve to continue its journey.

When the soul has experienced nothing so far except the diffused presence about which we have spoken, God may, with one stroke, rend the veil that was hiding Him. Then the soul's eyes will see far beyond itself and will look into the depths of the divine abyss. In an instant, God can make it grasp the mystery of the Trinity, His love, His Incarnation, His Passion, His hidden life in the world. The whole universe will seem to have been wiped out, as if it had been completely absorbed into God; for a moment, it will disappear into His light, only to reappear transformed by that same light.

As we remarked before, these graces sometimes come to the soul like meteors in the sky, but little by little they become part of the continuous evolution of the soul from the imperceptible presence of God to the prayer of quiet and ultimately to union. Certain souls receive more of them and others less, but this matters little. They are always valuable road signs for the soul on a journey that is often monotonous.

When a soul has marched forward for a time in the rhythm of the passing days in quiet fidelity, God can make it glimpse the intimacy with Him which it has achieved. The soul sees God; it sees itself in God and Him in itself. With one glance, it measures the road it has traversed, just as the mountain climber can pause on a height and look back over the whole steep path up which he has labored since he left the plain. Thus the soul goes forward, sustained by God's lights and graces.

At this point in its journey, the soul truly lives with the consciousness of God's presence in the world and, most especially, in itself. It has entered that degree of union in which it is conscious that this union is indeed an act of love, a reciprocal gift, in which each gives all that he is.

Chapter 19

In Loving God, We Love All Men

The soul still has one stage to traverse, the last one, which we shall describe in the next chapter. When the soul arrives at this, the highest point of its earthly existence, it will not be thereby lifted above the world and separated from it. On the contrary; the more the soul advances in the knowledge and love of God, the more it enters into communion with its fellowmen and with the entire universe. It is even true to say that, in the deepest union with God, the soul regains its connaturality with all creation.

It would be very superficial to think that, once the soul has found God, it returns to men because of a feeling of pity or compassion. The soul does not stretch forth its hand to its brothers simply because it feels a divinely inspired love for them, but because, in discovering God, it discovers the intimate bond that binds all creation together. In its relationship with God, it rediscovers its relationship to all creation in the One Source from which both it and the whole universe sprang. The second commandment, which many people keep only out of obedience to the Lord, is rooted in man's relationship to God, and that is why it is identical with the first and flows from the very nature of the creature. It was not just added on.

Authentic love of God cannot therefore kill the love of man in us. If what passes for the love of God is not joined to love of others, it is because it is only a conventional love, a selfish love that loves God merely for its own sake and not for Himself. True love of God, which we assume the soul has now attained, is, at the same time, love of men; they are one and the same love. Many persons, when they see young people consecrate themselves to God, think that they are incapable of love. That could be the case; some are afraid to love. But normally, he who gives himself to God does so out of a desire for a greater love, one that is deeper and more universal, a love that knows anguish and tears.

When a soul begins to devote itself to what are usually called "the exercises of the interior life," it is terribly tempted to turn in upon itself precisely because it thinks that virtue consists in applying oneself to these exercises. If the interior life is not, from the very first step, an opening up to God, the soul is burrowing into a subtle egoism, which will draw it on, turn it back upon itself and tie it up so tightly that it can't move. It will think only about its own problems, its own salvation, its own interior peace. The majority of souls pass through this egocentric phase. If it is only superficial and temporary, there is no need for anxiety, but if it continues, the soul must pray to God to intervene and turn everything upside down. Only He can lead the soul to concentrate on Him and, at the same time, open it up to the love of all men.

It often happens that, when a soul begins to feel itself strongly drawn by God into silence and solitude, it can no longer demonstrate its affection for those around it. It would like to do so, but cannot. Its inner eyes are turned toward God alone, and its anxious search for Him has the effect of making even the most ordinary conversations stilted and unnatural. It lives in the world with the feeling that it doesn't belong there any more. Everything it hears seems hollow, like a conversation overheard when one is half-asleep. It is awkward, clumsy and self-conscious. Everybody notices its constrained behavior, and for a soul that is naturally affectionate, this is one of the greatest trials of the spiritual life.

During this time, God is preparing for it a heart as wide as the world. The soul must pass through this period of inability to demonstrate love in order to find true love. God does not fix man's heart on Himself to turn him away from loving his fellowmen but on the contrary to teach him how to love.

The love of God cannot therefore serve us as an excuse or pretext for turning away from our brothers, and yet that is indeed what sometimes happens. If the soul does not discover love in its contemplative life, it is because it has not reached God. It is fixed upon an object that is a caricature of God, an idol, which is perhaps simply itself.

God calls the soul to love. This is the final point of contemplation, the communal action that engages God and man in the reciprocal gift by which creation is perfected. God did not create the world and man for His own glory. It wasn't worth the trouble! He created them only in order to associate man with Him in an act as similar as possible to the act of love in which the life of the Trinity is perfected. God's creating expresses the generation of the Word, and the slow return of creation to its Source expresses the return of the Word to the Father and their act of love, which is the Holy Spirit. Therein lies the key to our whole life.

All of creation is engaged in this expression of the mysterious generation and love in the Trinity. Everything comes into it, both joys and sorrows, successes and failures, because everything, in the end, tends toward that personal act of the gift of God to man and of the gift of man to God. The exultant joy of life and human love can carry the soul to God or turn it away from Him; and a divine love that surpasses all other loves can be offered to us in the very thwarting of our dreams.

What is certain is that he who has touched God in that act of love turns then toward his brothers with a new love which is the expression of God's immense love and which therefore knows no selfish limits or pettiness. God is love, and He gives love.

Chapter 20

The Saint in the World

At the stage which the contemplative has now reached, we can call him a saint, for that is, in effect, what he is, or else he has come all this long journey and has spent his time in building up a spiritual world in which he is not involved with every fibre of his being. That can happen, because there are spiritual lives built on a false intellectual contemplation which is the fruit of a keen mind and not of the love of God.

With the aid of the light and strength of God, the saint has traversed the inner spaces of his soul. Now his eyes see beyond the heights and depths of his own being. He has travelled through the whole world as Christ did and in His company, to enter into a divine intimacy with Him.

Now he knows and sees how the universe came from God. He knows it without understanding it, like everything that he knows about God, because the fullness of his knowledge shows him the non-existence of that knowledge. He knows it, and he advances in joy between the two abysses of unknowing and knowing. Finally, everything is resolved in union with God, and, in that act of union, he attains his own fullness.

In God he has grasped that moment outside of time when God placed the world over against Himself but not outside Himself. In God, yet over against Him and distinct from Him, this world derives from Him both that resemblance to Him and that independence of Him that will one day allow Him to demand a return in love.

We cannot say that there are no mysteries remaining for the saint. Yet he has penetrated all appearances and illusions to grasp everything that exists, minds and souls as well as everything else; and as far as his eyes can reach, in every direction, up or down, to the right or to the left, in front or behind, at the center of everything he always sees God. He finds himself with God at the center of all things and everywhere else besides. He is at that eternal point from which creation springs. The elements of imagination that get mixed in with this presentation can make him think that it is illusory, but it is not. In its reality it is the action of man united to the action of God in creation. Obviously, man received everything from God in the creative act, but the creature, in the very act of God that creates it, responds with all its being to God's action, as does the Word. That is where man's role in creation begins, and this role becomes more and more important as man grows in consciousness of it. The saint is always with God in an act in which the past and future are present, and in which he understands all creation.

In the world of men, the saint participates in divine charity. There is no person that is not present to him, none who does not share, in him and through him, in the mystery of God's mercy and love. We would be astonished if we could see the action of the saints in the world. Saints such as the Little Flower and so many others before and after her, great saints who have been popular with the faithful for decades or generations or even centuries, have worked wonders for all to see. But the other unknown, uncanonized saints have done the same things without anyone's knowing it. These are the ones who sustain the world of men, who give courage to those who are in despair and who turn back to God those who have turned away from Him. These men and women whom we are too often inclined to regard as being cut off from the world are really the closest to all mankind. But they are close to us *inwardly,* and that is why they seem to be apart.

The great problem for him whom God asks to devote himself to Him and to renounce human love, is to love with a true love those whom God places near him, and those whom He sends him, without having that love appear as the mere dispensing of an uncaring pity that is more interested in its own action than in the person concerned. If human love is a gift of self that impels us to love another for himself, how much more must the love of God teach us to love others for themselves, just as they are, with all their defects and all their hopes. The saint can love every man, and every man can find in him one who understands him.

If the saint has penetrated everything, pierced into the heart of everything, and has embraced everything in the manner we have just described, he is the only one in this world who is truly free. No longer is the world a hostile place for him. Even matter itself is no longer an obstacle for him to the knowledge of God, because he can see in it God's presence and action. He receives everything that the world brings to him as a witness to God's love. He sees God's life at work in everything that exists, and is well aware that the whole of creation is in labor, bringing forth a new world that will attain its perfection in God. Man is the great artisan of this new birth, and that is why the saint is not about to preach absenteeism from this world that needs him to perfect itself. Although he seems to have withdrawn from the mainstream of the world, the saint reappears in its depths.

He has penetrated the mystery of creation and of action because he has touched God. He can cry out to men: "Help creation to bring forth sons of God!", because, after all, it is through humanity that creation is raised to the honor of begetting and forming these sons of God.

Chapter 21

In the Trinity

The saint who lives among his fellowmen, just like anybody else, eating, drinking, praying and working in the world of men, leads his inner life hidden with Christ in God. That is his secret, and it has taken him years of slow progress and sudden illuminations to reach that point. When he looks back over the road he has travelled, he is amazed that he was able to do it. Without Christ, he would have done nothing, but would have been able only to lose himself in himself and find nothing but himself at the end of a completely human effort. He is unable to explain, even to himself, how it all came about. What he does know is that his life is hidden in God, in Christ, and that that life is a sharing in the divine life of the Trinity.

Christ was the voice that called outside the door, and He was also the door itself and the path, the vehicle, the movement and the power that set everything in motion. He was the beginning, the middle and the end, an end what will never finish.

In Christ and through Him, man enters the world of the divine life. The saint lives in perfect awareness of what the average Christian sees in faith as a mystery that is either too deep or too far removed for him really to grasp. While the saint cannot say that he sees the Trinity or understands it, he does live with the Trinity's life.

In the Trinity, he is a son, because he has entered there with the Son, and with the status of a son. He participates there in the eternal generation of the Son, because it is this grace of sonship in the Son that makes the Christian. When God shows man what He is, he grasps in himself the divine life that comes from the Father and flows into the Son and into all those who are sons in this Son.

Remaining always in the Son, in union with Him, in an act that is joined to the Son's act, he takes part in the breathing-forth of the Spirit, in the act of love that joins the Father and His Son, and in that act, which ranges as far as God's love can reach, he embraces all the souls that God has created for such a love.

The saint does not experience this only once or twice in his whole life, like something that can be felt only in a sublime ecstasy. Instead, it is the very essence of his supernatural life, and he is very conscious of it, although most Christians are only dimly aware that they share in God's life in some way. He understands and sees that the Trinity is the very mainspring of his supernatural life. What could be simpler than such a life, when we see the way in which Christ, while still on earth, used to speak about His relationship with His Father: "My Father is at work; my Father has given me. . . ; my Father has sent me; I love my Father. . . , and I always do what pleases Him . . ."? Nothing is simpler than the expression of the divine life in the Trinity, because that life is always simple, terrifyingly simple. The only thing that is complicated about it is our way of explaining it.

Although there are stages in the spiritual life during which the soul is blinded by the mystery of God, and although there are long stretches of night and desert, the definitive entry into union with God is luminous and simple. The soul may have a sudden flash of enlightenment when God reveals to it the secret of His personal life, but then it lives familiarly with Him. The mystery of its life of union with God does not frighten it but is as simple and natural as life on earth.

At the highest degree of union with God, the soul can be totally lost and absorbed in Him. The simile of the fish in the sea is really a very feeble comparison, since the soul is in God as a spirit in a spirit, a life in the life that animates it. Yet, for the soul, this losing itself in God is a discovery of what it really is, a being created to become God's intimate friend and co-worker for all eternity. Those mystics who regard losing self in God as the supreme degree of divine union stop short there. They believe that the stage of personal union is a lower stage of supernatural development. They want to be united to the Absolute spread throughout the universe. It is true that there is a first stage of the spiritual life in which man develops personal relationships with his God; and then he apprehends the divine in him and loses himself therein. This is part of common Christian experience. But the point at which man loses himself in God is not yet the peak of human development. God takes man, closes his eyes, and makes him lose his awareness of what he is by plunging him into Himself, and then, after this experience which allows man to understand his participation in the divine nature, God shows Himself to man in His inner life, His personal life in the Trinity. Then the love that was impossible when the soul, immersed in the divine nature, was becoming conscious of its obscure sharing in that divine nature —that love goes on to blossom out into the revelation of the mystery and life of the Three Divine Persons. Ordinarily, however, non-Christian mystics stop at the impersonal union of natures, in which love can expand no further.

The soul, therefore, becomes more and more conscious that it is in God as a person. In its union with the Son, it attains its ideal resemblance to the Father. In this sonship, it receives the perfection of its personal life, and when the life of the Christian has reached this intimacy with God, it no longer knows death, for death is then only a threshold beyond which life will stretch into eternity. The soul will continue to discover God, to lose itself totally and absolutely in Him, and als[illegible] become increasingly like the Son—and all this in a [illegible] of love that never stops receiving and giving.

But that is for the next life. Our saint, when he has arrived at the highest point of his union with God in this world, waits for the life to come and meanwhile tries to awaken his fellow-men to the mysteries that make up his own life on earth.

Part Two
Contemplation

Chapter 22

Gazing on God

Contemplation is gazing on God; it is the ecstasy of man in the presence of his God, the ecstasy of the creature in the presence of its Creator. All contemplation is based on this essential and natural movement of the creature who, becoming aware of what he is, turns back toward his source.

When contemplation is defined in this way, it may seem beyond the reach of most souls, but in reality this definition invites all souls to understand that contemplation is not a pious exercise in which one's degree of success depends on fidelity in following certain methods. Contemplation can be as natural for the soul as a child's gazing on its father and mother.

Gazing upon God, which is the essential act of contemplation, is not an act of the imagination or an intellectual representation based on good theology. Rather it is an act that is so rich that it cannot be expressed in any of the terms that are used to describe it. It is this gazing of the soul that, like an echo or a mirror, reflects back to God the gift of being and love which He has given to His creature.

Hence this gazing is not confined to any one faculty of the soul, but is in the soul's whole being. It is the return of my whole being toward God, and it expresses my position as a creature in the presence of Him to whom I owe everything that I am.

This definition is simple because it is fundamental. Why

should we bother with partial definitions which, by embroiling the soul in useless complexities, hold it back from attaining essential contemplation?

I know that the soul must advance step by step because it is travelling over difficult terrain, strewn with innumerable obstacles. But before starting out on any journey it is absolutely necessary to have a very clear idea of one's destination. Only too many souls engage in contemplation without knowing what it is; they advance with painful slowness, without light, often straying far, following inexperienced teachers.

This gaze about which I am speaking is only an imperfect image of that which the Word turns upon His Father, the gaze of a Son, by which He contemplates His origin and pays homage for all that He is. What the Son presents to His Father is not beautiful thoughts but His whole self.

When a man enters contemplation, it can only be in order to give himself back completely to his Source and his Author, like a mirror that is both reflector and image.

This act ought to be as natural for man as his joy at being alive on a beautiful spring morning; and to perform it, we need only become aware of what we are in the presence of our Creator.

However, as we shall soon see, this contemplation is not a simple gaze directed toward God. Rather it makes us enter into Him and see His unfathomable depths. This capacity for seeing God comes to us from Him, and our contemplation is achieved only in His light and with His power.

Chapter 23

Dialogue

The soul's lingering gaze upon God is a dialogue at the level of being, not a desultory conversation or a mere exchange of pious remarks, or even a blissful ecstasy; rather it is the expression of the essential relationship that unites us to God. God expresses Himself in us, though less perfectly, it is true, than in His Word. Nevertheless, we are made in the image and likeness of God, and, in contemplation, this image gazes upon its Source.

In order to understand what this dialogue is, we must relate it to the dialogue of the Word with the Father. God enters into dialogue with His Word, that is to say, with this expression of Himself, who differs from Him only in so far as it is He who utters the Word, while the Word is He who is uttered.

The Word uttered and produced by the Father expresses Him perfectly: the Word is the perfect, total expression of the Father. In understanding Himself, the Word understands the Father. Jesus said to His Apostles: "He who sees me, sees the Father." And what are we to say about the knowledge that the Word has of the Father in knowing Himself? By knowing Himself, the Word knows the Father perfectly.

The dialogue between the Father and the Son is so real that, in expressing Himself, the Father gives Himself whole and entire, and the Son gives Himself back completely to His Father. The dialogue thus engaged in is the dialogue of the

Participants' whole Being; and our dialogue with God should be like this, due proportion being guarded, for it is from Him that we have received everything that we are, since we have been created by Him in His image and have been made sharers in His Nature.

If our gazing upon God is empty and disappointing, it is because it is not sustained by this profound dialogue, of which the Father and His Word give us the example, and we are doing little more than exchanging words and looks, full perhaps of the highest sentiments yet empty of real commitment of our very being. In our contemplation we surrender little more than the outer skin of our personalities, and often even those personalities are false ones which we assume whenever we start to pray. Thus we are offering to God merely some beautiful thoughts that we have picked up here and there in spiritual reading books; but where is the frank gaze which reveals us as we really are?

Under such conditions, the gaze that we turn upon God can be little more than a vacant stare, an expressionless look that does not meet the challenge in God's eyes. And then we are surprised when we get nothing out of our contemplation! We shall get something from it only when, in dialogue with God, we throw ourselves heart and soul into it, as the Word surrenders to the Father all that He has from Him, all that He is, the Word.

If we are to arrive at that point, our gaze upon God must tear our hearts out. Otherwise, contemplation is only a parlor game, played according to its own rules. All our talk is only lip service, and all we offer of ourselves is some nail clippings.

Christ has shown us in His life how His gazing upon the Father and the Father's upon Him is continual, the natural expression of the perpetual dialogue that binds them together, that turns them totally one into the other, so to say, in a complete, reciprocal gift.

In everything, the Father expresses Himself, and that is His Word; He gives Himself, and that is His Son; and the Word-

Son gives Himself back to His Father. But isn't this a monologue rather than a dialogue? No, because the Father is a father, and the Son is a son; and what the Father is as a father, the Son is as a son. The Holy Spirit, the love which unites them, is identical with the Father and the Son, but as Spirit.

We know that we are children of God, and with this knowledge, we can go forward from light to light. A day will come when we shall see God as He is and we shall be like Him. He who starts out on the path to contemplation can immediately see, in faith, how this transforming gaze will make him like God.

Chapter 24

The Gift of Being

We are what we are because of a gift from God. There was a time when we did not exist, when nothing existed except God. Indeed, we cannot even say with strict truth in this context: "There was a time . . ." because time did not then exist, but that is of little importance since we can always say that there was a time when nothing existed, in order to express the fact that everything that exists has come from an act of God's will.

Things exist, and we do, too; that is the only fact that really poses a problem. How does it come about that things exist? *How?* This is the essential question; the "why" is only secondary. And there is no answer to this "how." Existence, our own and that of everything else, is a fundamental fact, and we know that the very roots of our existence, as well as those of the universe, are inaccessible to us.

The Being that existed first must have existed always; but the word "always" has no meaning before the existence of time. "Always" is only another way of expressing omnipotence, the power to exist of oneself. If there ever was a possibility that that Being would not have existed, He would never have existed.

But this Being does exist, and that is what concerns us here. He came from no one but Himself. But we come from Him, and we are not He; we are not a part of His Being placed in new conditions of existence. We are not particles of divinity shot into a space which they create by entering it.

God has achieved the astonishing feat of putting us into existence without our being He; but we exist from Him and by Him. God has given us being and life, and this being and life come from Him as completely as they can without being He. We are not God, and no matter how far we can go in identifying our existence with God's, there always remains a fundamental difference between God and us. We cannot extend the doctrine of union with the Divine to the point to which the *advaitins* of Hinduism push it. (The *advaitins* are those who profess the doctrine of non-duality—*advaita*—of the Absolute and the soul.)

We do not believe in a simple non-duality. Instead, we believe that we come from God in a duality that is founded upon an intimate communication of the gift of being, in a communion of life. God allows us to share in His life, not by means of a non-duality between His life and ours, but through creation. These are the facts which give Christian contemplation its essential form and which condition its exercise.

The basis of contemplation is the gift which God gives us of His life, and the continual flowing back of that life toward its Author; without this constant returning to God, human life loses all meaning. In its deepest roots and in its superficial areas, in its essential unity and in its rhythms, life must be in harmony with the relationship to God about which we have just spoken.

Only too often our contemplation consists merely in fixing our mind's eye on the idea of God which we have fashioned for ourselves. It is also fatally easy to stop at and contentedly dwell upon the feeling of a power that surges up from the depths of our being. Mere awareness of the life that is in us can make us think that we are touching God. Of course, God is in that life, and He gives that life its power and strength. But here we must aspire to a more mysterious grasp, in the depths of self, a grasp of this Being whom we call God and who gives us life. Faith guides us beyond ourselves in order to place us in contemplation before this source from which flows every particle of energy that is in us.

Perhaps this is not the way contemplation is presented in manuals on the spiritual life; yet contemplation should lead us to this discovery of God in our lives as men. God Himself is the object and the aim of contemplation.

That is where the problem lies, and it is complicated by the fact that, while searching for God, we cannot find Him unless He wills it. We can understand ourselves by an intuition, but, if God refuses to reveal Himself, we will not find in this intuition any vista opening on to the mystery of God. But God, by allowing Himself to be sought, has already opened up a path to those who seek Him. It is sufficient for the soul to recognize humbly that it cannot find God without His light.

Chapter 25

With All My Heart

I must enter contemplation with all my heart, just as the Word contemplates His Father with all His being. Every fiber of my soul, every faculty of my mind and every power of my body must be brought into play in this total contemplation.

Contemplation manifests itself to us in our minds, and this is so because the mind is the center, the focal point, of our awareness of what we are and of our knowledge of everything that happens in us. By the light of our minds, we present outselves to the Lord in an act of perfect self-awareness.

Because of this awareness, we are able to see at once the whole of our being as men and everything in us that resembles God. All that we have and are comes to us from the Spirit of God and is diffused from the initial point of creation; and it all tends to come together once again in the Spirit, in God, through Christ. Man's mind knows and is aware of this, and that is why the mind of man is the mirror of his contemplation.

There are forms of contemplation which require the mind to detach itself from created things in order to concentrate, to gather together within it all its forces and to go beyond itself by rejecting everything, even itself, if that were possible. This development of contemplation cannot take place without doing violence to the basic structure of human nature. Actually, as we have just said, I must put my whole being, my whole heart and soul, into the act of contemplation, and if I collect my thoughts, if I draw apart from all creation, it is only the better to unify myself within my soul. But I cannot be there where I am not, and I cannot reach a place to which I do not have access by means of some act of my own. That is why I cannot contemplate God without already being in Him, at least by an act of faith.

My body suffers when it is caught up in the movement of a contemplation that carries it far from its sense-faculties; my imagination suffers from being reduced to silence or delivered over to the disorder of its own turbulence; and my intelligence suffers, too. But even in their suffering and distress, my mind and body participate in my whole being's total contemplation.

In the exercise of the highest form of contemplation, my whole being is involved in an act of inexpressible simplicity; and the whole "me" must be active because the whole of me, body and soul, comes from God. The bond between my body and the living God, who is a pure spirit, is more difficult to grasp than the bond between my soul and God. But what would my body and all other material things be without this bond that binds them to God in their very existence?

If I am present to God only by means of an abstraction of myself, what good is such a presence? How can that vital dialogue we have mentioned take place? Yet those who have experienced this encounter with God know quite well that they are present before Him totally, fully, in a unique act which is man's response to God's creative act.

This act is one of total presence to God. When it takes place in all its perfection, it allows man to grasp how he comes from God and lives in Him. It is the most profound experience that man can have. It is his awakening, his enlightenment.

Like every experience of this kind, it is incommunicable. What, actually, has man seen? He has seen God in His creative act, and this sight, in the present order of grace, cannot already be a glimpse into the inner life of God. But it is, in fact, impossible for man, in this apprehension of the divine action, not to see that this act is love: "God so loved the world that he gave his only-begotten Son . . ." (Jn 3:16). But God's creative act was already an act of love performed in view of that even greater act of love which is the gift of His Son, the Word who expresses the whole of God for man.

For him who has thus laid hold of God, life is, in a way, completely new. His life is changed through its having attained its source. The power of God, perceived in the simplest conceivable act, shows itself in everyday life as a power that is, at the same time, immense, all-embracing and all-penetrating, and also as the simplest, most condensed and most concentrated one possible. It is, at once, both total immensity and a point without dimensions, one which, nevertheless, contains all the power of existence.

Chapter 26

In Myself, Yet Beyond Self

There are methods of contemplation which, by turning man's efforts toward himself, become an obstacle to his contact with God. Such methods prevent the contemplative from realizing that in discovering himself as he really is, he cannot but discover the bond that links him to his beginnings.

By positively denying every bond with the Creator, these methods hinder the contemplative, despite all his efforts, from grasping the hidden presence of Him who is the source of all existence. It is then almost impossible for the contemplative's own practical experience to overcome his false intellectual conviction that such a presence cannot exist. It is a fact that experience never imposes itself on the one who has had it in terms that the mind can enounce clearly. Jacob wrestled with the angel but discovered only later that he had been in contact with God.

Then, too, it is not surprising that the contemplative who has attained the highest point of his spiritual experience should think that he is identical with the Absolute, for it is in this same experience that the Christian mystic discovers his likeness to his God. What the one mystic will interpret as confirmation of his theory of the *advaita* (identity in non-duality), the other will see as that state of perfect union in the distinction of persons that is fully realized only in the Trinity.

This experience of plenitude that can make us believe that we are the Absolute comes from the fact that we are creatures. This plenitude, the plenitude of the divine that man can achieve, would be an insignificant thing for God. The oyster which can see no farther than the edge of its shell can believe that it is as large as the sea; but if it knew that it encompassed only an infinitesimal part of the ocean in which it is immersed, it would still have the same feeling of plenitude although it recognized its smallness in the ocean which overwhelmed it by engulfing it in its immensity.

In somewhat the same way, the Christian soul sees in itself, in what it can contain of God, the whole Absolute that encompasses it. If it sees itself as enlarged to the dimensions of the Divine Being, it does so only because it believes that it is in God, completely changed into Him, but without being God.

In contemplation, the soul grasps the fact that it is more than itself. When it attains the profound meaning of its existence, it discovers that this existence, in its origin, in the forces that animate it, and in its destiny, is truly more than itself, because God is everywhere in it. God is everywhere in it, and yet it is truly its own human existence. By touching the very principle of its existence, the soul discovers that God is there. And God is there, not as a completely foreign power, but already so mingled with human existence that man has meaning only in God. Apart from God, man does not exist and can have no meaning. This is what makes man so much greater than he is in himself. He is not merely himself.

Here man finds himself confronted by a great mystery, one which could be relegated to the scrap heap of things which it is futile to investigate if it were not vital for him who draws near to God in contemplation.

In the Trinity, the Son's total dependence on the Father makes Him the Son and not the Father. Similarly, in his dealings with God, man realizes himself most fully as a person in his most intimate relationships with God. The more clearly he sees that he is dependent on the source of his existence, and the more he makes himself so dependent, the more he grows in real freedom. The contemplative mystic is fully aware that it is in this dependence that he attains supreme liberty.

This consideration can shed light upon our Lord's declaration that He is equal to the Father even while He affirms that His Father is greater than He. He knows everything that His Father knows, yet there are things which only the Father knows. In His total dependence on His Father, the Son is greater than any son can be in his relationship with his father. Man, who is so tiny before God, is greater than himself in his divine sonship.

Whichever path the contemplative may follow in his contemplation, if this contemplation is in conformity with human nature, the contemplative will discover in himself such extraordinary riches that he can only call them God, or the Absolute, or the One. By penetrating to the foundations of self, he discovers that he is not the foundation of all things. He finds in himself Another who gradually takes over all his dimensions until he is swallowed up, and then he enters into ecstasy before this Other; he is captivated and captured by this Other, by Him whom we call God, the Father of all things.

Chapter 27

In the Light of Faith

When a Christian begin to search for God in contemplation, he knows, from Christ and the Church, who this God is whom he hopes to encounter at the end of his journey. His path is lighted up from the start by the light of faith which revelation gives him.

Hence the experiences which the Christian contemplative has during his pilgrimage are continually controlled by this light of faith. When St. Teresa of Avila began to perceive the presence of God within her, she asked herself if she wasn't suffering an illusion. The first spiritual advisers to whom she went for guidance were ignorant men who only increased her bewilderment. It was not possible, said they, that God should manifest His presence in that way. Finally, however, other more learned theologians reassured her about this form of the divine presence, the reality of which she was beginning to apprehend directly. The saint submitted every new experience to outside examination, so that she was able to advance in the light of faith and under the direction of spiritual teachers who themselves had felt the presence of God.

In his climb toward the heights of contemplation, the Christian finds footholds in the teaching of the Church and in the direction of those who have traversed the same route before him. And it is remarkable to see how spiritual souls, while guiding themselves by the light of faith, acquire a sense of

God that allows them to appraise His action in other souls. They themselves are being guided in this very same way, instructed by other teachers and enlightened by faith.

For those who have not experienced it, all this may seem like a dream world in which it is very easy to get lost. But I think that, of all mystics, the Christian mystic is certainly the one who can advance with the most assurance because he is not left at the mercy of the pure subjectivism of his own impressions and experiences. Every experience that he has of God contains elements that allow it to be verified. Sometimes, perhaps, such verification requires the skill of a great contemplative, but the important thing is that the Christian's journey along the paths of mysticism is a journey in light, even if the soul finds itself in the blackest night. Faith does not die, and its light always remains, even in the desert and in the night. We can even say that faith shines with a brighter light as the darkness deepens, just as the light of a star is more brilliant as the night grows darker.

The light of faith is necessary at all stages of contemplation, and it will cease only in the Beatific Vision, in the next world, when we shall see God as He is and our apprehension of Him will be immediate. But while the soul is still on its earthly journey, faith helps it to see more than it grasps. In the Beatific Vision, we shall no longer need faith or hope, and only the love that unites the soul to its God will remain.

Therefore, while the soul is still on its way to God, it will always need faith. It is faith that lights up the road before it, illuminates from afar the paths along which it must pass, and it is faith also that clarifies its spiritual experiences and gives them their depth.

When the soul says that it has evidence of the presence of God, this evidence is always clarified by faith. When God shows Himself, when He acts as Lord in the soul, faith may no longer seem so very necessary; but since God never shows Himself except in signs, faith must still be exercised to give these signs their full significance. Faith is always there to throw its light on the sign that God uses to make His presence felt. Faith uncovers an abyss in the soul itself, opening up in it, and beyond it, the perspectives of the divine life, with a glance that is penetrating, intuitive, as quick as lightning and as decisive as a laser beam. The sign is penetrated and volatilized in the divine light which flashes forth in the wake of the act of faith, and the soul loses itself in the intoxicating joy of an incomprehensible love that is revealed by that flash of light.

Thus faith, the flickering candle by whose light the contemplative ventures to take his first hesitant steps, will also be his guiding light on the summits of the mystical life. In the soul's sudden illumination by God, faith itself seems so radiant with divine light that it appears to be nothing but light. Yet, although faith is transfigured, it remains to the end, if only to act as a guide once more to the contemplative in the blinding divine light of the final stages.

For many contemplatives—indeed, for most of them—faith remains the only light that shines upon their path. Direct lights from God are often so feeble to the eyes of the soul that they serve only to shed new light on the teachings of the Faith, making it luminous to man's eyes and warm to his heart.

Chapter 28

The Power of Grace

From the very moment a Christian sets out in search of God in contemplation, he knows that he is not being left to his own devices, and he certainly cannot say that he is relying on his own capabilities. The One for whom he is searching is the very One who is giving him the strength to search for Him. The moment he takes his first step forward, he is already caught up in the current of God's life, and is already in Him for whom he is searching and, in Him, advances toward Him. This is a great mystery, yet it is quite clear to those who have experienced it.

God is unknowable and can be known only if He makes Himself known. And He is known only in and by His own light, a light that has come to search for man in the depths of his night, that strange light in which God hides Himself with all His brightness.

God is inaccessible and can be attained only by the gift of His own power. And this power is fully offered to man in the first movement that he makes to take his first step toward the Lord.

At the end of his long journey, the contemplative will be able to say, as he looks back over the road he has travelled: "From my first glance, from my first step, God was there with me, and I didn't know it!"

Anyone who tries to raise himself up to God is deceiving

himself. He cannot say: "I will force open the door of God's mystery!" Nevertheless, the humble contemplative can say this with all truth because he knows how to recognize the fact that he has reached God. Yes, he reaches Him with all the strength of his soul immersed in His strength.

The non-Christian who knows that he is incapable of reaching the Supreme Being by his own powers, by that very fact finds that he has already been enlightened by divine grace. However, this enlightenment may come to him deformed by the religious education that he has received, and he can be mistaken about the way in which God enlightens him. But one thing is certain, and that is that God *does* enlighten him.

The position of the Christian is completely different from that of the Buddhist monk of the Hînayâna ("Little Vehicle") school for whom there is no God. The efforts of such a monk to reach *nirvâna* are completely human, and the whole success of his striving toward contemplation depends on him alone. His concentration and his final victory in reaching the point where he is empty of all desire are both his own personal achievement. Under these conditions, Buddha can only lead his disciple to the borders of the unknowable and cannot make him penetrate the mystery of that unknowable as Christ does by the revelation of His father in Him. In the indefinable state known as *nirvâna,* man can no longer be a definite entity, for he no longer has any personality. He does not emerge as a person in the love of another person. He does not apprehend, because he himself is not apprehended. Who is there to understand him? There is no one to transform him at the end of his journey, and there is nobody to help along the way. This is the great loneliness in the lone man's striving.

The Christian contemplative, too, advances into his soul, for there is no other place into which he can advance. In thus advancing, he discovers that he is advancing into God and by the power of God. In discovering this power of grace within him, sometimes concentrated in a prodigious intensity and at other times spreading out in infinity, but not diluted, he understands that his personality can find both its unity and its immensity only in God.

If a Buddhist does have a real experience of God's presence, he is almost certain to lose the benefit of it by the denial of God which his faith imposes on him. For the Christian, on the contrary, even the absence of God reveals His presence. He knows by faith that God is always in every one of his actions and that his activities are always within the divine activity.

Therefore the Christian acts in constant relationship to God's action. He takes a step toward God, knowing that he does so in God, and if he acts with reserve, it is not through fear of action, but in order to show that, by faith, he sees God acting in him. By his reserve, he shows that, while his action is truly his own, it is especially God's in its being put into effect. This is not because one part of his action is his, while the other is God's. His action is both God's and his own, to two different degrees of being, an action that is common to two different, more or less profound levels of efficacy.

Chapter 29

Effort and Grace

For many authors the essence of the spiritual life seems to consist in methods and effort, as if God played almost no part therein. The person who follows this school of thought can build up for himself a spiritual life that is perfectly regulated and easy to control but in which progress is liable to be halted because of an excess of confidence in human efforts. Such exclusive attention to methodical effort would be understandable if everything depended upon man. And it actually is understandable, in a climate of faith in God, for those temperaments which need such control in the minutest details of their contemplative progress. If the object to be attained is the greatest concentration possible, it is necessary to use proven psychological methods such as are practiced in Zen. These methods can be utilized in Christian contemplation, but with the restriction that they lose their value because of the single fact that the Christian contemplative, in his personal striving, is attentive to a divine action that comes out to meet his own.

By using the appropriate exercises, I can succeed in placing myself in a state of almost total emptiness, thereby liberating my mind. I can grasp that profound relationship with all things which makes my personality expand to embrace everything that exists. But I have not thereby attained that Divine Being who is the great "beyond-myself", except in the sense that I have reached His presence in created things. But Christian contemplation, by the manifestation that God makes of Himself, gives access to a knowledge which is God's taking possession of the soul and also a personal relationship with Him. Contemplation attains its perfection only in this union with God in which the soul finds itself immersed in Him in a union which throws into bold relief the personal relationship. The development of contemplation can be understood as the emergence of the Personal God from the Impersonal One by which He first reveals Himself to the contemplative.

And this divine action, which, in the end, show itself with all the radiance of the midday sun, is already at work from the very beginning of the contemplative's journey. He knows by faith that this is so, and that is why, in every action that he performs, he reserves a place for the action of His Divine Partner. He is always aware by faith that his own actions have value only in the divine power that animates and guides them, and this changes completely the perspectives of a mysticism that can be called natural.

We can see why certain schools of contemplation, such as Zen, have developed their methods so greatly and why, very early in the Christian contemplative's journey, his own action gives way to God's. In Zen, methods can lead the soul to the outer limits of human knowledge, but then the *satori,* the highest degree of illumination in the discipline of Zen, is reached in an inexplicable way. (The term *satori* is taken from the language of Japanese Buddhism.) This idea springs from consciousness of man's ultimate relationship with everything that exists. Thus the basis of being is revealed, a point which merely human effort can attain.

But Christian contemplation surpasses the quite profound relationship revealed by the *satori* and goes on to set foot in the Absolute of God. Obviously, man can do nothing toward making this last leap into the Absolute. But the soul has been making this leap into the Divine Absolute from its very first step along the path of contemplation, in simple, naked faith.

The Christian does not set out simply to delve into something mysterious yet intriguing; the mystery that he is trying to unravel is God Himself, who reveals Himself to him who is searching for Him. There is a knowledge of the Trinity that the learned theologian can possess, one which he can have acquired by his own intellectual efforts. But there is also a simpler, deeper knowledge of that same Trinity which God Himself bestows.

Contemplation is not the contemplation of dogmatic formulas, but an insight into the mystery of God in a dialogue that involves man's whole being. God gives Himself by expressing Himself to the soul, just as in giving His Son to the world He expresses to the world all that He is, for this Son is His Word.

In his long journey, the contemplative will begin by doing his best to exert every effort in his search for God. At the beginning, despite the faith he has in God's action, it seems to him that he is acting alone. Then, little by little, God's power will allow itself to be seen through his efforts. And the day will come when God will seem to take over all man's activity. Man will enter that new phase of the spiritual life in which God acts openly and puts the soul into the passive state which is proper to mystical contemplation.

Chapter 30

God Invades the Soul

No matter how human and natural may appear the methodical progress that leads the soul to God, it is already animated by grace, because no human action, much less man's progress toward God, can exist without God's action. At the beginning, God does not show Himself any more than He shows Himself in the growth of plants or in the ordinary actions of men. Nevertheless, it is His profound activity that gives existence to everything that exists and motion to everything that moves.

The contemplative reflects on the mystery of God and tries to understand and savor it; and he does all this by faith. Yet this spirit of faith does not change his method in any way but only directs and vitalizes it in its application. And this is how the contemplative's search ordinarily begins.

The soul knows that its action has meaning and value only when immersed in God's action. God urges the soul to seek Him at first in the knowledge that He gives it, by faith, of His greatness and perfections. He can thus give it a taste, an attraction, that will render the exercise of contemplation appealing to it. That which hitherto seemed tasteless and illuminated solely by the light of faith will become full of a mysterious delight. This may seem completely natural, although it is already the manifestation of a very special action of divine grace.

Thus the soul may find a profound delight in thinking about the mystery of the Holy Trinity. Intellectually, it knows no more than before, but it is happy in meditating on the mystery of the union of the Persons, on the manner in which They communicate with each other in the unity of the Divine Nature. The understandable content of the Faith takes on a new dimension when knowledge of it becomes more enchanting and hence more concrete and direct. This zest may be nothing more than an attraction, a certain joy or interior relish, yet this is sufficient to change completely the soul's apprehension of the mystery of God.

A psychologist will explain this in a natural way, but the natural explanation on the level of analyzable reactions does not exclude the reality of God's action, which works on a more profound plane and wells up to the level of consciousness. That which appears in the conscious mind rises up from the depths of the unconscious. But given the body-soul structure of man and his immersion in the divine, it must be admitted that there are sources deeper than the unconscious. That which comes from God may appear to us as coming from the depths of our psychological life, but, with the help of a light that originates beyond us, we know that it comes from Him.

While God's ordinary action may remain very circumspect, and while He may normally show Himself only by touching the soul lightly, He can also invade it suddenly. We can find, rising up from the depths of consciousness, feelings that bear the mark of God's presence. These are the clouds that ascend from the bottom of the abyss and conceal that presence.

The intensity of these manifestations may lead us to believe that they originate in the most profound depths of the soul. It is true that that is where they are formed, since they have no form in God; but that which these feelings, these ideas, these intuitions, express comes from beyond. Ordinarily, the soul hesitates when confronted by the first manifestations of this type; and it says to itself: "It's only my imagination!" But when the content of these manifestations is revealed, the soul understands that God is showing Himself in this way.

And God can thus rise from the bottom of the soul or from the depth of man's nature. How or whence He comes is of little importance; the soul knows that He is its God, and that is enough for it. It knows that He is there, showing Himself in a mysterious way. In the beginning, it used to think that it was experiencing a more intense, more interior form of recollection, but then it saw that the best way to describe the phenomenon was to call it a presence or a face. Someone else was there, Someone who gradually loomed larger and made Himself known and acknowledged as the Other, that great Being who is the human soul's one and only true Friend and Companion.

One day, this presence will be so overpowering and this face so clear that the soul will be able to do nothing but remain before it without moving a muscle, saying a word or even evoking a thought. God will occupy the whole field of its consciousness and vision. He will have taken it over competely. And the soul will be in Him as it would have been if Adam had not sinned and as it will be in the Beatific Vision in Heaven.

Chapter 31

From Activity to Passivity

At first, many souls think that they can, as it were, squeeze the divine action into their busy spiritual schedule. They imagine it is their efforts that matter in meeting and apprehending God. But God does not let Himself be taken in this way. He is the Master of His manifestations to the soul, and He does not allow Himself to be either enticed or waylaid. He guides the soul toward Himself although it may not be conscious that He is doing so. And it is a great mistake to believe that God permits Himself to be caught in the net of our meditations or by the television cameras of our contemplation.

Ordinarily, God allows the soul to take its first steps toward Him with the help of the most usual methods of meditation and contemplation. The soul then feels that it is directing its own spiritual life, and it makes progress in proportion to its efforts, which gives it great self-confidence. Unhappily, some souls settle down in the feeling of security that a well-regulated, perfectly controlled spiritual life gives.

Then a day comes when God decides to detach the soul from the superstition of its ways. He turns its beautiful spiritual abode upside down and makes it understand that the essential thing is not its activity but its docility to His guidance. Gradually, He teaches it the secret of true dependence. Then it becomes docile to grace and discovers the power of God's action, before which it will soon be able to do nothing but submit.

The development of contemplation is therefore divided into two periods. During the first, human activity becomes interior and simplified. The divine action scarcely shows itself except occasionally and briefly. God is invading the soul without showing His face, by sending it inner lights and deep attractions. All the soul's prayer seems to develop on the natural plane, tending toward a greater and greater simplicity.

It is usually only when contemplation has become very simplified in form and content that the divine presence begins to show itself. When prayer has become very simple, such as in the prayer of simple regard or simple repose in the presence of faith, there appears in the soul a new element, a new imperceptible presence, which is so tenuous, so slight, so circumspect, so close to absence, that it is almost impossible to distinguish it from that mysterious perception which accompanies the knowledge derived from faith.

Soon this presence becomes clear, and the soul suspends its thoughts and its movements in order to give all its attention to this compelling presence, this growing gleam, this swelling melody. This presence sometimes seems to surge up from the depths of the soul's being, while at other times it seems to appear in that indefinable place in the soul or in the universe in which it lives. Nevertheless, for a long time it can only be a gleam in the night on a seemingly endless road over a monotonous plain, a gleam that seems never to come nearer but which, for all that, is there, quite close.

If the soul is faithful in its attention, this presence will increase. But the soul must have the courage to suspend its own activities and to stop weaving its own ideas out of the shining threads of light it receives. It may have to wait for a long time until the gleam of presence shows its origin. It may have to remain for months, perhaps for years, with the unfinished work lying on its lap, waiting for Him who is present only in the night to show His face and to speak to its heart. The soul's prayer remains suspended between a past activity that no longer has any reason to exist and God's taking it in hand, which has not happened yet.

For most souls, this is the time of great torment, nights and desert. The soul is waiting, waiting and burning with desire. It suffers from being outside of itself, outside the comfortable home of its own thoughts. It suffers at seeing itself still unworthy of being received into contemplation of the Lord.

It sweats away the poisons of its humanity, it disgorges its pride, it eliminates its vanity, sensuality and laziness, ridding itself of everything that cannot enter into the vision of God. Sometimes God, as it were, pounces upon the soul, burning, striking, hacking, pillaging, crushing and running it through. He must do this if the soul is still clinging to its possessions. And when everything in it has been washed clean, rinsed out, dried and passed through fire, God shows Himself.

Then God makes a gift of His presence. He sends an immense peace into the soul, consoling it, strengthening it, enriching it with virtues, enlightening it and revealing His love to it. He shows Himself to it and introduces it into His own divine activity.

The soul, having seen its own personal activity reduced to nothing, now beholds it taking on new strength and new breadth, but this time in the immensity of God. No longer are its horizons its own but those of God. No longer does it recognize any limits. As if it were the most natural thing in the world, the soul goes by itself to the depths of God and extends its love to the whole universe of souls. It lives and acts in God, to the dimensions of God and in the power of God. No longer does it act of itself but is activated by God; yet all of its activity is truly its own.

Chapter 32

The Torments of the Soul

It may all seem very simple: a conscious, well-controlled activity which gradually gives way to a take-over by God's action; a contemplation whose field of operation becomes more and more concentrated until it loses itself in a point of unutterable simplicity and which slowly spreads out to the dimensions of the vision of God; a life that delves ever deeper into its contact with Him.

This would all be very simple if man were not man, and God were not God. Man does not accept so easily the necessity of losing himself in order to give himself completely to God, for that is what he actually experiences when he feels that he is losing command of his own life and becomes aware of God's increasing hold on his soul. He is not always disposed to accept without a struggle God's invasion of his life. He knows that this invasion is going to play havoc with the human equilibrium that he has so patiently achieved and to which he clings fiercely. Up to this time, God had given him his independence, with its accompanying pride and self-esteem, but now He is asking him to blend and lose it in a higher and more intimate union.

God cannot but be a torment for man. Man is man, limited,

restricted, and normally shut up within his own horizons, and God must break down the walls of that little private world. Even the saints felt anguish at God's approach, and besides, God is so very "other" from us.

Even the saint is gripped by God's "strangeness," yet he loves and rejoices at being taken captive by God. But what about the man who sets out toward God along the paths of contemplation weighed down with the burden of his rebellious humanity? He feels free, with the freedom that God has given him, as he well knows; and he wants to remain free, in the pride and self-esteem of his intellect. So much for his mind; but what about the complaints and the outcry of his body? And even when all his fleshly desires have been controlled, there still remains his independence of mind that makes him like God.

With the call to union in silence, emptiness and simple presence, the soul's great torment begins. The purifying trials of the first stages, those which man directs against himself, are nothing compared with those which overtake the contemplative when God shows him His face for the first time.

Only God can carry out the purification which the soul needs before it can enter passive contemplation. It used to be able to pray, meditate and contemplate, while still being full of defects. But now its deep-seated attitude of self-sufficiency and independence is incompatible with what God wants to accomplish in it.

God first attacks its independence, but although He wants it to be docile, He does not wish it to be shapeless. On the contrary, He wants it to become more personal in its dependence on Him than it was in its former independence. In order to raise it to this degree of freedom, God must destroy in it the false liberty it built up for itself in its independence; and to do that, He may have to torture it mercilessly, reduce it to nothingness and destroy in it all possibility of false self-esteem.

God does not crush the soul for the pleasure of hearing its bones crack. All He wants to do is make possible that liberty that the soul must possess if it is to be capable of accepting joyfully all His action in it. What breaks the soul is simply God's love, for He wants to have a being that is as free as He —if that is ever possible for man—to share in His love.

Of all the torments, the most terrible is that of the divine darkness, which begins from the moment God shows Himself to the soul, when He prepares it for a kind of knowledge that is different from the simple knowledge of faith. Therefore, like the torments described above, it is caused by the nearness of God. The first torments were necessary to prepare the soul for His coming, while this one accompanies that coming itself. The purified soul finds itself even more alone, even more left to its own devices at God's approach. This new torment attacks the soul in its highest faculties and not in its more sensory ones, as before. It sees that it cannot make itself "capable" of God. His approach blinds and crushes it, even while giving it great joy. God appears so far above its powers and faculties that it is reduced to silence and to powerlessness. His light blinds it, and His greatness shrinks it to nothingness, yet it knows that it is loved. Its torment consists in not even being able to receive all the love that God is showing it.

The soul desires God. It knows that He loves it, it tries to raise itself up to Him, but it understands that it is incapable of doing so. It is not a question here of gathering one's human forces, of pushing them to the extreme of effort; this only makes more evident God's inaccessibility. He allows Himself to be glimpsed, to be desired, but He leaves the soul with a terrifying feeling of powerlessness, in darkness, emptiness and disgust. Yet the very keenness of this torment reveals the intensity of God's advances. If He were far off, the soul would never have been subjected to these torments. The soul's torments here are the result of man's nature and of God's; it is the meeting of these two that produces the torments and that, one day, will transform them into a union of perfect joy between God and man.

Chapter 33

Purification in Depth

Contemplation is not a matter of intelligence or imagination, but is, as we have said, the engagement of our whole being in a heart-to-heart dialogue with God. It takes place on the deepest levels of the soul, for that is where the divine action meets its only real obstacle, the soul's radical desire to escape God's taking possession of it, a desire from which spring both rebellion and sin.

It is true that man can fight against his evil tendencies by his own efforts combined with the assistance of grace, but he can do practically nothing against the powers buried in the deepest recesses of his soul. He cannot descend that far into himself and come to grips with himself in those mysterious forces which are the source of his activity.

Even psychoanalysis must remain incomplete because it cannot go deep enough to reach the point where I am placed by God in His presence as His image, capable of entering into a dialogue with Him, and where, at the same time, I remain so much myself that my normal tendency is to close myself up against God by asserting my personality. Beyond the multiple influences that have contributed to making me what I am and that come from many directions—from my heredity, from the environment in which I have been reared and shaped—beyond all that there is this center of unity that makes me *me*. In last analysis, this is what makes me who I am and no one else. And this is the source of that self-will and pride which Lucifer showed in his outright rebellion against God and which Adam and Eve allowed to develop into their disobedience.

In its successive stages, contemplation helps the soul to become aware of the unity of the person. It eliminates secondary elements and concentrates the soul upon itself, revealing to it its basic unity. In discovering itself, the soul sees that it is rebellious against God, and it relies upon Him to purify it in its deepest tendencies. I have said that the soul relies upon God, but quite often, it is afraid to have God purify its inmost depths.

Ordinarily, God begins to purify the depths of the soul before it has become aware that such depths exist in it. When God is purifying the soul, He seems to be working at the bottom of a very deep well. The soul itself can do nothing. It finds that it is reduced to silence, that it is dumb and incapable of taking the smallest part in what is happening in it. It begins to feel a dull pain deep within it, and it knows that its most precious possession, its independence, is going to be taken from it. It is like a patient on the operating table, who knows that they are going to open him up, to search for and cut out a tumor, but who has only a vague idea of what the surgeon will do.

Often the soul is kept in ignorance of what God is doing deep within it, but sometimes it does have a dim perception of His aim. It seems to it that He is burning, cutting, slashing, grinding and crushing it. The work may go on for weeks or months, because the soul must lose the smug self-confidence and independence of God that is its most fundamental attitude.

When God has finished this work, the soul will emerge from the trial washed clean and emptied of self. It now understands that its independence, its true independence, is built on dependence on God's creative and vivifying act.

This is a difficult point to understand, yet it is essential to a knowledge of the spiritual life. We receive everything from God, and our dependence on Him is what places us in His presence as persons worthy and capable of love. This dependence gives us all the power and riches of God. Thus we become true creatures of the Lord of all things, who enables us to possess everything He gives us, not as greedy and envious plunderers, but as loving sons who are at home amid the riches of their Father.

This purification of the soul's depths reaches so deep within us that it prepares us for the contemplation of the whole of being, which is true contemplation.

Chapter 34

Sin and Contemplation

The real obstacle to contemplation is not the difficulty of recollecting oneself or of looking with the inward eye on a representation of the mystery of God, but rather the persistence of a deep-seated determination to resist God. This is not a passing, intermittent whim, but something that involves one's whole being.

That is why, when God has changed the soul down to its very depths and turned it completely toward Him, it can have no other definitive will but His. It can will with its whole being only what He is and what He wills. If it does happen to commit sin, it can do so only by an act which, though gravely sinful, does not involve its whole being. Its will is then involved in the sin only superficially, as it were, and its fundamental allegiance to God has not been affected. It has faltered and stumbled, but it recovers its balance, almost in the very act of falling.

Hence, when a soul which God has taken over completely happens to fall through weakness, it gets up again as soon as it comes to grief. Often the soul sees the evil of its sin and bitterly regrets it at the very moment it commits it; in the very act of sinning, the soul sees the perversity of sin.

If the soul acknowledges its sin and repents from the bottom of its heart, God shows it even greater love than before, and it discovers a new dimension in Him and in itself as a result of its sin. Certainly, any sin that affects God's most intimate relationship with us makes us very conscious of our own greatness by showing us our ability to reach out and touch Him by an act of sin.

In repenting, we discover that "God is greater than our hearts" (1 Jn 3:20). When we have sinned, therefore, we should not allow our heart to close in upon itself but should instead let it open out to the dimensions of God's love.

However astonishing this may appear to some "just men," sin does not inevitably stem the flow of divine graces, and God often continues to give great mystical graces to souls which are still weak but which He wishes to bring to perfect love of Him. A soul of this type is already completely turned toward God, but it is not thereby protected from sins such as those we have just mentioned. It may give in to the allurements of the flesh or to pride, but it does so only in a fleeting moment of superficial weakness. God knows well how strongly pride and sensuality draw man away from the love of Him. He knows what every man knows who has felt the violent tug of his own self-love against the love of God.

In order to understand the Lord's love, we have only to watch how He acts with some souls. He wants them and already possesses them, but sometimes they still prefer, as passing fancies, other joys and liberties to those He offers. He then watches and waits, helping the soul in its struggle. He knows that, if it does give in to evil, it does so only out of weakness, a momentary weakness that does not really separate it from Him because its will to sin is not the fundamental will of its being.

And God keeps on giving generously to these souls, bestowing on them as much as He can. He gives them still more light on His Nature and more joy in their union with Him. Thus He makes the soul understand that there is in it a power other than the one whereby man wishes to assert himself. He enables it to grasp the fact that there is a love and, in that love, joys greater than any the world can give.

In its sin, the soul discovers its essential weakness. When

it falls, it is thereby so torn interiorly that an abyss suddenly opens up within it, but one in which it finds its God.

The path I have just described is truly a mysterious one. It leads the soul a long way toward the discovery of love, but it is a painful path, one on which the soul also discovers its own frightening wretchedness and, in that wretchedness, God's incredible love. If it accepts God's help, the soul will emerge victorious from this trial, and a day will come when it will enter the intimacy of God's love once and for all.

Contemplatives are often tormented by terrible temptations in mind and body, both of which rebel when God introduces the soul into contemplation. The mind rebels when it discovers something greater than itself, and the body revolts against being forsaken. It can happen that some instincts, such as the sexual instinct, run amok when no longer controlled by reason, which itself has been subjugated in contemplation. Sometimes the imagination may feel that it is completely submerged in a flood of carnal thoughts and sensations. The whole sense-life is affected, and by a gesture, even by a mere unspoken consent, the soul could give itself over to the pleasure that is coursing through its veins. It does not want to do so, and although its whole being may be plunged into pleasure, it resists being carried along with the floodtide. It does not desire this pleasure, but deep inside its human nature a joy is welling up, inundating it but without penetrating to its inmost self. Something in the soul is revelling in pleasure, but whatever it is, it is not the soul itself.

Thus a soul can go through all that without being in any way besmirched by it. God's presence in the soul has bound its essential will to His. It belongs to Him, it is in Him, and everything else is nothing but surface agitation. God has taken possession of it, and it wants to respond to His love by giving Him all of its love.

Chapter 35

The New Love

Contemplation renews man to the inmost fiber of his being because it redirects his profoundest powers and the most secret sources of his activities, as well as giving him a new insight into his most natural forces.

What seems purely natural to us, has, in fact, a spiritual root and a spiritual aim from the moment it begins to play a part in man's fulfilment. This is true of the sexual instinct, as well as of man's other instincts, and if people understood the profound meaning of sex, they would be filled with a holy fear. It is this instinct that ensures humanity's advance toward its completion, which can be attained only by slow development over successive generations. No other instinct plays a more necessary part in God's creative plan.

When a person renounces this creative power, it can only be in order to unite himself to the creative power of God at a deeper level, and union with this divine force, which is closer to the source of being, enables him to participate in a vaster and more universal divine power.

Basically there is no opposition between union with God's creative power in human love and union with this same power by renouncing that love. But in actual fact, human love is so demanding that, only too often, it become an obstacle to full union with God. Hence the difficulty of attaining and expanding, in God, even the most fundamental requirements of human love induces many people to renounce that love in order to ascend alone the stream of creative power to its source.

In the new man whom contemplation should create, all powers are redirected and developed in order to reach the dimensions of being itself. He even feels an overflow, as it were, of this profound conversion in every nerve of his body. It would be too much to say that many people arrive at this point, for unhappily it frequently happens that efforts at contemplation never go beyond a small, closed-in universe, a false spiritual world, which may reach the dimensions of piety but certainly not those of God.

The saint is one who has penetrated into, and then explored, the depths of his own soul with the help of God's light. There he went down into an abyss of night and of death, until the day when the divine light made everything clear by purifying him. In that light, he came to see how, although he was the product of the long line of his ancestors stretching back behind him, in the last analysis he was bound to God by an even more intimate bond.

It is this bond that makes him capable of turning completely toward God. Because his freedom is very real, although sometimes rather precarious, he can go to God directly through everything that makes up his contingent being. Thus he ascends the stream of creation to reach the Creator Himself, and he has the first and fundamental experience of the creature who grasps the Creator's primary act, the act of love, which has given existence to everything that is.

In this divine love, man also discovers the other dimension of creation, not the one which reaches down into his own heart to his first moment of life and his first breath, but that which extends horizontally, beyond the reach of sight, in every direction, to wherever other human beings live and move. Like him, each one of those beings has a bond with God, but how many of them know it?

In God, in His love, in His primordial act of love, an act that is always going on, the contemplative has discovered this new dimension of himself which unites him by a fraternal bond with everything that exists and most especially with all men, in the brotherhood of the sons of God. The heart of man, which is thus at the center of the universe, beats with one and the same love for God and for his brothers.

If he has never chosen anyone in particular as the recipient of his love, he is reproached for not loving. It is true that he cannot love as do a man and woman who give themselves to each other, but he does love, and loves as much as they do. And although his love is not the one that men seek, it is not thereby any less love. The love which two human beings have for each other is the reciprocal gift of self in bodily union. But it is never merely that and can never be merely that. The love which is manifested in the union of bodies infinitely surpasses that act of union. It is that love which the spouses are, in last analysis, seeking, and which is so difficult to achieve fully. This human love is a spark of the great love that comes from God and animates all creation.

It is this divine love that the saint is seeking to lay hold of, and when he has attained it at its source, beyond the manifestations of carnal and spiritual love, he can thenceforth love only with a universal love.

This love is none the less real for its being "spiritual" and universal, for it is not an abstract love, but one that is terribly demanding and concrete. Nor is it a uniform love, applied to everyone indiscriminately, because, although the saint loves his fellowmen with a universal love, he also knows how to love with a personal, unique love those whom God has bound to him with a special bond. This love must be measured according to the dimensions and depth of God's love. And God loves His creatures with a love that embraces them all and touches them to such a depth that He alone knows their secret. But the saint, in God, can reach that point.

Chapter 36

A New Vision of the World

What we have just said about the new dimensions of love shows how the soul that has reached the intimate knowledge of God opens out, seeing the world with new eyes, seeing its immensity both in depth and in extent, and penetrating the world of souls, which is the soul of the world.

The soul sees how everything comes from God, remains dependent on Him, and lives by that dependence. The world no longer seems to it like an autonomous universe, yet it discovers that the world is freer and more master of itself than before. This world is put into being for its own sake, since it is the greatest beneficiary of its own existence. However, at a deeper level, it was created for God alone. The ideas "for man" and "for God" are no longer opposed to each other in this new vision of creation. The paradoxes which present-day philosophers find in the very idea of existence vanish with the deeper insight which is revealed by God's own light.

In this new vision, what concerns man most especially is that he sees how God has ordained all things so that he may know and love Him. Obviously there is another way of explaining creation since God has willed that the universe be an entity that exists by itself, but this independence on the part of the universe is only an appearance. Those shortsighted people who judge things by outward appearances alone walk through the world completely at ease. And God is not going to rise up from the depths of His creation to demand that men should reserve a place for Him in His own universe. He must be found everywhere but at such a depth that it would be too much to ask our superficial philosophers to dig so deeply.

That's the way it is with man. He can explain himself by causes and by causes of causes. He can build up around himself a world that seems to hold up perfectly by itself, but in thus explaining himself, he forgets the essential thing, namely, his origin and final destiny. He comes from God and returns to Him.

Since man, by himself, never succeeds in seeing beyond himself, God came among us to explain the details of our relationship with Him. In the God-Man, man discovered the divine dimensions of his human destiny, and light, as brilliant as the noonday sun, is given in the clarity of faith to those who are willing to investigate this mystery of the Word of God expressed in the life and words of a man.

But the contemplative wants more and seeks, in a personal encounter with God, to experience those things which faith reveals to him. It is not in any way that he doubts the truths of faith, but he does wish to experience in his human nature God's presence in the world. He does not seek so much to grasp the ground plan of all things as to enter into personal contact with the Word, who will open wide to him the doors of the mystery of God and of the world. He is searching for God, and God will make him see all things in seeing Him.

Man knows that, in God, he will see the divine plan with the eyes of God. For a long time his journey will be an arduous climb, a slow ascent, up the side of the mountain of knowledge of God. He will advance at his own quiet pace over the first slopes and will wait at the foot of the steep cliffs until the Master of the mountain comes to guide his steps and help him climb the precipices. Often God will blindfold him and lead him over impossible paths along which no man can travel alone and unaided.

As the soul ascends the winding path up the mountainside, it can look back and see the plain stretching into the distance beneath it, and it will discover there new horizons. God will enable it to climb so high, to the culminating point of the universe, to the highest peak of the highest mountain of the soul, that it will see itself and all creation in one glance.

The soul does not merely see farther through the eyes of God but is itself transformed, becoming more and more like Him according as it discovers more about Him. A day will come when it will know as much about Him as man can know, and, in that very knowledge, it will see its own capacity for knowledge growing continually greater. In discovering more about God, it becomes more capabe of Him. This is the way it will spend eternity, in an ever greater discovery of a God, the knowledge of whom makes the soul capable of ever greater knowledge. Thus new capabilities for an ever greater love are created in the soul, and this begins even in this life for him who has found God.

The man who has reached this new vision of the world can no longer judge the things of the world as he did before. It is not that he is absent from the world, nor that he is living in another world, but simply because he sees everything from within and not from the outside. He no longer sees things set out in front of him and merely bound together by visible ties. Instead, he sees all created things in depth, in themselves, in the depth of the existence which God has given them.

Thus he sees how that personality is formed in man which makes him a being like God and capable of Him. Beyond all time elements and all the vicissitudes of the evolution of created things, he sees how this universe came from God and can return to Him. Then there will no longer be any earth, any world, and yet they will still be there, in God. God knows how this can be, and man has an inkling of it.

Chapter 37

In the Word Made Flesh

There appeared on earth a man who was God Himself, the most fantastic event in human history, which, while it leaves the unbeliever very skeptical, becomes increasingly real in the eyes of the believer. For the contemplative, the truth of this event is more and more evident according as he advances in the discovery of God, for it is, in fact, by and in the Word made flesh that man discovers the way to God.

The great problem of mystical contemplation is precisely the truth and reality of this contemplation. Can the mystic really reach God? All the great religions pose this problem, and many are the answers and the approaches to it.

The Christian has the certitude of faith that he can reach God in Christ, who said: "He who sees me, sees the Father" (Jn 14:9), and this is so because the Son is in the Father (Jn 14:10) and because the Father and the Son are one (Jn 10:30). The problem is to see Christ in depth. Many people have seen Him only superficially and have taken Him for a man like every other man or, at most, for a prophet, whereas the Apostles, for example, came to see Him in His profound reality, and thus they saw God in Him; therefore, they saw God.

The stages of this discovery are simple and within the capabilities of all sincere souls. It is not necessary to practise extraordinary asceticism or to spend long hours in contemplation. If a person loves Christ and keeps His commandments, he will receive the Holy Spirit, who is God like the Father and Son—not another God, but another Person in God. If he loves Christ in this way, the Father will love him, and the Three Divine Persons will come to dwell in him. When Christ returned to the glory of heaven, mankind in general could no longer see Him, but those who believe in Him will see Him again, for He said to His disciples: "But you will see me; because I live, you will live also. In that day you will know that I am in my Father, and you in me, and I in you" (Jn 14:19-20).

What more does the Christian need? Everyone who believes in Christ can see and touch God through faith, and, for the contemplative, this life of faith will shed light on God and on himself. Here the most perfected methods of contemplation pale into insignificance. Not only that, they are burdensome to man, and there is a danger that they will divert him into himself without finally leading him to the Other, who is God.

There is a mysterious path that leads from every soul to God, and souls who thirst for the absolute have always tried to follow it. There is an order of things that we call natural and in which man stands in relationship to his God, his Creator and Father. If God has created man out of love, it is inconceivable that He should not have given him the means to reach Him by a path that is hidden in the very foundation of human nature. We know that this fundamental relationship to God is infinitely mysterious, and that is why human thought has erred so much in its search for God. But this effort on the part of so many souls has not been in vain, because many of them have certainly sensed God in Nature and in their own lives, and have reached out and touched Him.

The great religions have offered a thousand ways of getting

in contact with God. Here human imagination has tried every way possible to reach God through the pathways offered by the forces of Nature. The beauties of the universe, the vitality of living things, the creative instinct, love, thought—all have served as symbols and vehicles for attaining God. Some people have sought Him along the path of the forces that animate Nature, while others have searched for Him in human consciousness and the human mind, renouncing everything else. Even the atheists are looking for Him.

Unfortunately, man's search for God has often led him along perilous ways. Wise men have arisen to point out the road that leads to Him, yet all they could do was indicate the path of wisdom and teach their own method of following it. And, indeed, many people followed their directions and drew close to the Creator, the Mother and Father of all that exists.

But none of these teachers was able to bear witness to God Himself. Christ alone claimed to be both God and man, and vindicated the faith in Himself that He demanded. He bore witness to God and gave man the means of reaching God—in Him and by Him. Through Him alone come total mediation and revelation. The other great religious founders have their place close to Christ, but there can be only one Word made flesh.

This Word made flesh is the focal point of all human history, and all other mediators and prophets will converge in Him. Naturally, this will take time, but it will come about. History reveals how the world is built up, but it does so slowly and at its own pace. All religions are the way of salvation for those who practise them, but there is only one definitive Savior of mankind. In the religious history of the world, Christ and His religion are the great central point of evolution upon which all other faiths will converge.

Men save their souls in and through their religion, but, in fact and on a deeper level, they do so in and through Christ; and the final consequence is that many will certainly be saved by Christ, despite their religion.

In Christ, the Christian contemplative possesses Him who is the final and definitive Pattern for man. When he has been transformed into Jesus Christ, he discovers himself, in God and divinized by grace. In Christ, everything that exists is open to him; he goes from man to God, and from God back to man. He lives his life as a man in God, as did Christ.

Chapter 38

In Christ Through Faith

In becoming man, God simply involved Himself more intimately than before with His creation. He was already involved with it since everything that exists derives from Him its being and its ability to feel and act. But in becoming man, He made accessible to men His personal life, which He was not in any way compelled to share with them. And His Incarnation did not affect man alone since all creation converges on man, and man on Christ. All creation, therefore, converges on Christ in order to be able to return to God by and in Christ.

In Christ, God offers man a new participation in His life, new because it is a sharing in His inner life. In this gift of God, there opens up a new way of knowledge which does not destroy the first one but rather deepens it, bringing it to a more fundamental, more divine level. Just as the revelation of the Trinity does not end by contradicting that of God's Unity but rather reveals its inner dimensions, this new knowledge that is offered to man simply deepens the knowledge that every man can have of God without faith in Christ.

The gift that God makes of Himself in Christ marks an extraordinary advance over the gift of existence bestowed in the act of creation. God gave existence to men without asking for their consent, but when Christ came into this world to reveal to them the path of God's love, He asked for faith in Him. He stands before men and asks: "Do you believe?" If I do believe, Christ communicates His life to me and opens up to me infinite horizons on God. This act of faith is the central point of the new order. It is an act in which man and God participate, and in it the two worlds are bound together, and life passes from God to man, bringing man into the life of God.

This act of faith is man's essential act, that by which he goes to meet God and joins in God's own action. Faith is a gift of God, and many people use this gratuitous aspect of faith as a pretext for saying: "I haven't the gift of faith, and it's no fault of mine!" This is true in one sense, but man's frame of mind is as important here as the offer of faith by God because God does not force his consent. It is also certain that God always gives man enough light, but man can always refuse to turn his eyes toward the light and can also retain habitually such a cast of thought that he will never be really aware that faith is being offered to him. The interplay of the human will and grace is so subtle that it is not possible to go more deeply into it here.

Through faith, the Christian cleaves to Christ, divine life is given to him and with it a new knowledge is offered to him. Faith itself is a type of knowledge, and thus cleaving to Christ in the act of faith becomes a gateway to the mystery of God. A new form of contemplation begins at this point, one which a soul that has not found Christ cannot know. In cleaving to Christ, the soul cleaves to God, and lives from and in Him. Christ becomes the center of its life in God and even is that divine life.

Contemplation follows back to their source the channels through which life flows, and therefore it penetrates to the depths of God. In Christ, God is given to us completely; He is completely open to us, completely manifested and completely expressed to us, and the remarkable thing is that, in this mode of knowledge, we do not have to climb the summits of thought in order to reach Him. In Christ, God has placed Himself on the same level as our earthly dwelling place, on the same level as the paths we travel every day, those earth-bound paths of our daily life. The Christian meets God as the son meets his father in their home.

That is why the very complicated methods of some spiritual schools have no place in this new mode of knowledge offered by Christ. It seems quite likely that it is precisely the absence of a doctrine of grace that has compelled these schools of spirituality to develop such exacting methods of contemplation. But their methods must of necessity be quite heroic because they hold that all progress in contemplation depends entirely on man's own efforts. However, such methods only result in discouragement for many souls because they often lead those who use them merely as far as the boundaries of self-knowledge, without really putting them in contact with God. And what effort, what self-control is needed to achieve results that are frequently very meager! Yet many souls do arrive at union with God by means of these methods, but because such souls lack light and strength, they are unable to attain the full flowering of that union.

The Christian contemplative's knowledge is only the radiance from the divine life that circulates between God and the soul. There is a current of divine life in every soul, but it is not as rich or as abundant as that which comes to us through Christ. The knowledge which the Christian has of God is supported by the divine life that circulates through his soul. This life re-creates man in the inmost part of his being, cell by cell, and it deepens, widens and develops fully his relationship to God by introducing him into the life of the Trinity. Man enters God with the Son and as a son.

The contemplative, therefore, plunges into the current of God's life and, making his way up along this current to its Source, he enters God. And this is not reserved exclusively for the great ascetics. Every man who sincerely wants to find God can gives his allegiance to Christ, who will take him into Himself in order to reveal God to him.

Chapter 39

Reaching God in This Life

By faith, God becomes accessible to us in all the actions of our lives. If we turn the eyes of faith upon our souls, we shall see there God's life in us. Every believer can experience this daily mystery, and to do so he does not have to go through very difficult and painful exercises of concentration and loss of consciousness, nor does he need to set himself down to contemplation in order to set out on the search for a knowledge that is being offered to him if he has the courage to leave behind his egoism and his self-esteem.

The efforts demanded by complicated ascetical programs, those of religions lacking in all savor and devoid of divine grace, are replaced by a total cleaving to God which is essentially nothing but leaving self to return to God. That is why the demands of the Gospel do not consist in outward practices but hinge on a deep change of heart, the word "heart" being used here to symbolize the deepest spring of human activity, that center of activity from which each man expresses his real self.

Hence the Christian does not always have to go through a long period of strenuous effort before he can hope to discover God, who offers Himself to him every day and in all his actions. The soul does not set out to seek knowledge as such. Instead, knowledge of God flows naturally from the Christian life. Christianity is not primarily a religion of knowledge but of life, from which everything else flows. The mystery of God is revealed to me in the union of my life with Christ. That is why Christ gives Himself to those who place their trust in Him by their act of faith and reveals Himself to those who obey His wishes. Cleaving to Him is the first requirement, since it allows life to flow from Him to the soul. Then knowledge of Him blossoms out into conformity to His will.

The ordinary knowledge which the Christian receives in his cleaving to Christ is knowledge in faith, which every Christian can and must have. But the contemplative seeks another kind of knowledge; he wants his knowledge through faith, which is already so luminous, to become experimental for him. He wants God's presence, which faith reveals to him, to become as clear and as visible for him as the close presence of someone very dear to him.

In the soul of the contemplative there develops a faculty for grasping the divine, while the divine manifests itself more intensely and, so to say, more palpably. One of the most mysterious features of the spiritual life is this possibility of grasping God in oursleves and in every created thing by faculties that are none other than our own human faculties. Under the influence of the divine light, those faculties of ours work at a greater depth and are then capable of intuitions which they cannot have outside of an intimate union with God's life.

When the soul advances along the paths of contemplation, new horizons open up before it. It sees how it is inhabited by God and worked on by Him; it sees the all-presence of God and His activity in all things; and it sees Him as it sees everything that exists, both the world and other men.

But only a soul that is detached from everything created, that is, one that does not stop at creation for its own selfish pleasure, can grasp God in creation. Since God is in all things, giving them existence and the ability to act, He is everywhere in the universe that surrounds us, revealing His power, greatness, beauty, charm and tenderness in everything that He has put into the world which He made for us. Seeing God in everything is by no means pantheism, and seeking to understand Him by gazing at the grandeur and beauty of His creation is not an illusion. The only danger is to make oneself the focal point of this universe. We are, indeed, the focal point of creation, but only as unifiers of God's wonders for the enjoyment of our fellowmen and the glory of the Lord of all things.

Many people have touched God in Nature, which has always been one of the preferred places for man's meeting his God. Man merely has to have his heart pure enough to recognize the signs of God's presence in the grandeur and beauty of the universe.

In finding God everywhere, the contemplative understands that it is not only in silence that He allows Himself to be approached. God is not solely the God of those who retire to the desert, but is also the God of active people, of those who live and work in the big cities. He is the great Worker of whom His Son, our Lord, said: "My Father is working still . . ." (Jn 5:17). God gives both existence and the ability to act, and both manifest His presence. That is why the contemplative finds Him as readily in the fever of action as in silence and tranquillity.

God undertook a great work in launching the world into existence, but who is going to finish building up that world? Must this astounding task be left to those who don't believe in God? God is waiting for Christians to set themselves to this task, and contemplatives are needed if the work is to be perfect.

Chapter 40

Contemplation and Action

The opposition between contemplation and action is a false one. Unhappily, only too many spiritual authors have written about this subject in such a way as to give those souls who are seeking contemplation a concept of action that is more likely to make them afraid than to help them.

If there is any opposition, it is between contemplation in idleness and action without any contemplation, that is, between action and inaction. The most genuine kind of contemplation can bloom in activity as well as in restful solitude; it can, therefore, be the flowering of action as well as the product of inaction. The non-action so esteemed and preached by Taoists is, in fact, an activity of a superior kind, even in the natural order, for it is a positive non-action which puts man into a state of active union with the active principal of all things, both in his repose and in his most strenuous activity.

In the practical order, there is a form of contemplation which requires withdrawal from ordinary activities and from the usual worries of daily life, but there is also a form of contemplation which flourishes even in the most intense activity. There are, of course, some people whose temperament cannot accommodate itself to any form of contemplation, but, in order to assess the problem, we must consider the broad spectrum of souls.

There are spiritual writers who advise their disciples to replenish their interior life during times of contemplation and to embark on action only very cautiously, while taking care, as St. Francis de Sales counsels, "not to give our hearts a shock." This advice can help many souls, but it must be taken in the spirit in which it was given. We must know how to pass from the most tranquil prayer to the worries and stress of our daily life with an ease that shows we are doing everything for God.

It is true that life today is full of dangers for what we call "the interior life," but contemplation gives us strength against the dangers we may encounter. It gives the soul what is known as a "supernatural view" of the events of life, but this view is unquestionably incomplete because in it action is not integrated with contemplation and does not itself become a contemplation, as it should do. Every other solution will always be shaky and will always leave the soul unsatisfied. It is true, of course, that the soul will be able to draw strength from contemplation, but since it is not well-informed on the very value of action for contemplation, it will see the strength and light that it gained in prayer draining away in activity.

If a soul does not clearly understand the real interrelationship between contemplation and action, the two will always be in more or less hidden conflict. In this case, however, action will be nourished by the grace of contemplation, lighted up and reinforced by it, and, as it were, "saved" by it. The contemplative soul will approach action with a very elevated view of God's glory. It will throw itself into the activities in which God wishes it to engage, with a very high resolve to do everything for the glory of God. In this way, the soul's activity will be sanctified more in its aim than in its reality, since that activity is considered to be, in itself, an obstacle to union with God.

At the bottom of such ideas as this there is a view of created things and of action which is widespread in many religions and which, from time to time, has seriously menaced Christianity itself. This is the idea that the world is evil and deceptive, a perpetual temptation for the children of God. Now, we know that the most formidable temptation for man is man himself. And, unhappily, many souls flee from the world and its clamor only to be devoured by themselves. They become the prey of a monster that consumes its victims slowly and inexorably. We must not consume, but rather lose, ourselves, for that is the essential law for finding ourselves in God.

For those who withdraw from the world in the way I have just mentioned, spirituality consists in retreat, flight and finally absence from the world. In their opinion, action hampers them and distracts them from God. And since this world must pass away, it can be only a very precarious prop, too unreliable even to help us on our journey to God. Hence it is better to leave it to those whose eyes are blind to its deficiencies, better to flee toward what is entirely spiritual. But this highly vaunted spiritual refuge may be nothing but a castle in the air. It certainly is not the world of God which faith reveals to us.

We know that God created the world and put man into it to finish out His creation. But man can turn to his own selfish profit what God asks him to perfect; the fault, however, does not lie in the created world but in man's perverse intention. This world offers man a marvelous field of activity, and if he looks at it closely, he can discover its Creator's basic intention and his own place in this universe that is being brought to fulfilment.

The coming of Christ widened even more the perspectives of this undertaking. God became man, thus changing the very conditions of contemplation. This world is not an illusion but is the world in which God took on a body. Christ is not a myth, and the world is founded on the rock of God's very firm and very real will. Man's heart allowed itself to be seduced into wanting to center everything on himself, so that he became locked into an infernal circle. But Christ came to free him therefrom.

In Christ, the Christian has found once more the true focal point of the universe and goes beyond repose and action. He sees everywhere the possibility of contemplation as repose in the consoling thought of God's existence and union with His unceasing action.

Chapter 41

Concrete Knowledge of God

I have spoken about contemplation and the divine life, about knowing and apprehending God. But what is this perception of God which man attains in mystical apprehension of God? When a man says that, in his prayer, he has touched God and has felt His presence, what kind of knowledge is he talking about? How does he know that he has perceived God and His action?

In certain spiritual disciplines, very elaborate methods are used to teach the disciples how to experience the existence of something beyond themselves, or at least to grasp by means of a unique intuition the fundamental bond between our existence and the cosmos or the absolute. For some souls, this experience is the fruit of a concentration of all their human energies on a point within themselves but situated on the very boundaries of our world. Man's activity is then so absolute in its simplicity that it cannot be described in any language. He understands himself in his beginnings and, at the same time, grasps his relationship with the world of the absolute, upon which he depends for his existence. Thus he can enter into communion with the forces of the cosmos, quench his thirst at the well-spring of all things, and unite himself to their Principle.

In the spiritual journeys of which I have just described some stages, man advances solely by his own efforts and powers. He does not receive any help from an absolute which, he believes, does exist but which is not a person (or Persons), and which has no concern whatever for those who are searching for it. There are, particularly in Hinduism, very rich spiritual doctrines, some of which teach how to rediscover one's profound identity with the Absolute, while others help souls to unite themselves with a God in whom they can lose themselves without thereby having their own personalities disappear. This latter form of Hinduism is obviously very near the Christian concept of God and His relationship with souls.

In the Christian view, man knows that he is searching for a God who loves him and who wishes to receive him into His own inner life after the manner of the Divine Persons. Man is no longer left to his own devices, and the Christian also knows that, at the end of his personal journey, he will not be absorbed into God to the point of not existing any more.

When man sets out to find God in contemplation, he knows that, dwelling within him, there is a divine power that has become the support and the environment of his spiritual activity. He knows this from his faith, which teaches him this mystery, and, in the knowledge that he derives from his faith, he both knows and sees it. In his faith-derived knowledge, the whole universe is built up before his eyes. But this vision is not a mere figment of his imagination, for although human images and constructs may be mixed in with it, its essential feature is knowledge derived from faith and based on the acceptance of God's word made intelligible in Christ. God alone knows Himself; God alone has seen Himself, and no one else has ever seen Him. He came to express Himself, and He has uttered Himself, explained Himself and shown Himself.

That is what forms the knowledge of God that contemplatives find in their contemplation, that and nothing else. It can be said that they know no more about it than the simple believer who believes with all his heart and tries to raise himself to a "lived" faith by doing what the Lord tells him to do. In all that, the believer has total certainty, and in this way he touches God, apprehends Him and unites himself to Him, actions which come from God, the Giver of all things, but which are also those of him who abandons himself. Faith is the framework upon which love is built.

When the contemplative discovers God's presence in the universe or in himself, this presence gives recognizable features to that which his faith has already known for a long time. His faith-derived knowledge immediately becomes concrete and palpable. Nevertheless, he possesses less certitude in his new form of knowledge than he had in his knowledge derived from faith. Yet he finds fresh confirmation of his faith in his new perception of God's presence because this manner of apprehending God is, for him, of the same order as his other forms of knowledge.

Over a long period of time, this apprehension of God may be simply an as yet undefined intimation of His presence. The contemplative will not understand who this Other is who is showing Himself. As long as the evidence is not provided, the soul will remain in suspense, asking itself: "Can this be God?"

Unless the soul receives a stronger light than this in the beginning, its new way of knowing God will only gradually reach the degree of clarity that will make the soul certain. And this new knowledge will not teach the soul anything, for it already knows through faith what it now discovers by direct knowledge. But the illumination given is new, as is also the savor that accompanies it, with the result that its knowledge is now more human, direct, concrete and appetizing.

The contemplative is embarrassed if he has to express what he has discovered. He says that he "sees" or "touches," but most often all he can say is that he "perceives." This perception is a comprehensive view of God, or the direct understanding of a mystery, or the certitude of a contact. These new types of knowledge add nothing to the data of the faith, for they are already contained therein. But in the wide world of the faith there appear areas in which the truths of faith come alive, where the mysteries become clear, and where the divine life emerges into the open. And all of this is happening because God is allowing Himself to be glimpsed.

Chapter 42

The Ineffable Language of God

When the soul has advanced sufficiently in the mystical life, God shows Himself to it in many ways. Nevertheless, for each individual soul He has a special way of making Himself known because temperament and psychology differ from one person to another, as do the particular civilizations in which each one lives.

Undoubtedly, the most frequent manifestation is the perception of God's presence, which, although it is one presence among others, is ordinarily of such a quality that it is not just another presence. In its most attenuated form, it is a presence and nothing more. It is perceived sometimes within the soul and at other times outside it; as being nowhere and everywhere; sometimes localized, confined to one place, and at other times without any boundaries. Often the soul finds itself so plunged into it that it is penetrated by it to the marrow of its being. It happens also that God's presence may be nothing more than an imperceptible point at the bottom of the heart, or a conviction in the mind so simple that it no longer seems to have any support but itself.

This presence may be perceived in the silence of prayer or in the midst of the most absorbing occupations. It is not to

JUL 2 '75

to hear His voice in all creation. The road that leads there is very arduous, but since God is guiding us, why should we be afraid of starting out upon that road? At every step we take, God is there.